AutoCAD
Productivity
BOOK

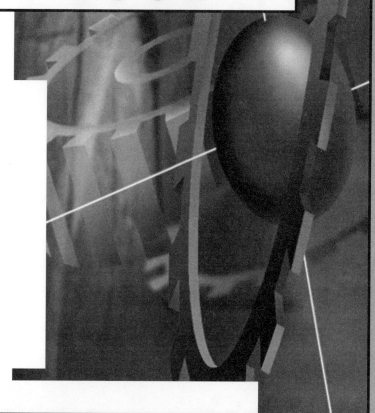

AutoCAD Productivity

BOOK

The
Non-Programmer's
Guide to
Customizing AutoCAD—
For Release 13
for Windows

Sixth Edition

James L. Brittain
George O. Head
A. Ted Schaefer

VENTANA
PRESS

AutoCAD Reference Library™

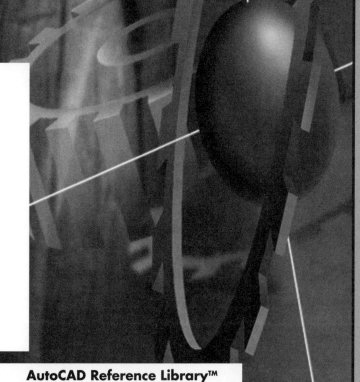

AutoCAD Productivity Book: The Non-Programmer's Guide to Customizing AutoCAD—
For Release 13 for Windows, Sixth Edition
Copyright © 1995 by James L. Brittain, George O. Head & A. Ted Schaefer

Library of Congress Cataloging-in-Publication Data

Brittain, James L.
     AutoCAD productivity book : the non-programmer's guide to customizing
  AutoCAD for release 13 for Windows / James L. Brittain, George O. Head &
  A. Ted Schaefer. -- 6th ed.
        p.   cm.
  Includes index.
  ISBN 1-56604-185-6
    1. AutoCAD (Computer file) 2. Computer graphics.
  I. Head, George O., 1945- . II. Schaefer, A. Ted. III. Title.
  T385.B76 1995
  620'.0042'02855369--dc20   95-6596
                             CIP

Book design: Marcia Webb
Cover design: Tom Draper Design
Cover illustration: Tom Draper Design
Vice President, Ventana Press: Walter R. Bruce III
Art Director: Marcia Webb
Design staff: Dawne Sherman
Editorial Manager: Pam Richardson
Editorial staff: Angela Anderson, Tracye Giles, Nathaniel Mund
Developmental Editor: Tim Mattson
Project Editor: Eric Edstam
Line Editor: Martin V. Minner
Technical Editor: Brian Matthews, Architectural Technology Dept. Head, Wake Technical Community College
Print Department: Dan Koeller, Wendy Bernhardt
Product Manager: Clif McCormick
Production Manager: John Cotterman
Production staff: Lance Kozlowski
Index service: Stephen Bach
Proofreader: Sue Versényi

Sixth Edition 9 8 7 6 5 4 3 2 1
Printed in the United States of America

Ventana Press, Inc.
P.O. Box 2468
Chapel Hill, NC 27515
919/942-0220
FAX 919/942-1140

Limits of Liability and Disclaimer of Warranty

Trademarks

Trademarked names appear throughout this book. Rather than list the names and entities that own the trademarks or insert a trademark symbol with each mention of the trademarked name, the publisher states that it is using the names only for editorial purposes and to the benefit of the trademark owner with no intention of infringing upon that trademark.

About the Authors

James L. Brittain, a graduate of Oklahoma State University School of Technical Training, has extensive experience on five CAD systems, including AutoCAD, and now specializes in writing LISP routines for CAD and computer graphics programs. He received the *Cadence*-sponsored "Top Gun Award" in 1990 and 1992, and is currently employed at Business Computer Center in Tulsa, Oklahoma.

George O. Head is president of Associated Market Research, a business and management consulting firm for architects and engineers, based in Rhode Island. He is a co-developer of A/E Solutions, a project management and financial accounting software package for architects and engineers and a developer of Auto Mechanical, a comprehensive mechanical AutoLISP program for mechanical draftsmen and engineers. He is the author of *AutoCAD 3D Companion* and *AutoLISP in Plain English* and coauthor of *1000 AutoCAD Tips & Tricks* (all published by Ventana Press), and author of *Managing, Marketing and Budgeting for the A/E Office* (published by Van Nostrand Reinhold).

A. Ted Schaefer is President of Schaefer Enterprises & Associates, an AutoCAD menu product business. He is an author, a consultant in system management and a programmer. His articles appear frequently in *Cadence* and *CADalyst* magazines. He can be reached at S.E.A., P.O. Box 5062, Mishawaka, IN 46546; 800/727-1726.

About the Technical Editor

Brian Matthews, department head of Architectural Technology at Wake Technical Community College, Raleigh, North Carolina, and director of its AutoCAD Training Center, has been responsible for organizing and creating courses in several areas of AutoCAD and AutoLISP application for the past nine years. His courses are taught as part of a two-year degree for engineering technology curriculum students. He has also been coordinator and instructor for several AutoCAD Industrial Extension Service programs at North Carolina State University. He was technical editor for all of the books in the Ventana Press *AutoCAD Reference Library*. Readers with technical inquiries can reach him at 919/662-3476, via fax at 919/669-3369 or via the Internet at bmatt@wtcc-gw.wake.tec.nc.us.

CONTENTS

APPENDIX
A

Using Text Editors **249**

AutoCAD—Out of the Box or Customized?

What is AutoCAD out of the box? It's a powerful, easy-to-use computer-aided design and drafting program that can be used "as is" by people with only an elementary understanding of CAD. Users at all levels can create professional drawings much faster with AutoCAD just as it comes out of the box than they could by hand.

Release 13 for Windows has gone even further to make AutoCAD the most user-friendly, interactive software that Autodesk has ever created. In doing so, Autodesk has not put every feature of Release 13 in the core program. In fact, it "customized" the existing program through the menu file, the .mnl file, the dialogue box file, the toolbars and other AutoLISP programs that are now as much a part of the program as the LINE command.

In the early days of AutoCAD, little could be done to customize Auto-CAD to specific needs. You could change the tablet menu a little, but that was about all. Over the years, AutoCAD's customizing capabilities have increased by leaps and bounds; today it's not only a great CAD system but truly a graphics engine and a complete operating environment.

What does this mean for you? Can you use AutoCAD as is, without investing a lot of money and time installing third-party software to modify the program? Of course you can. But look at it another way. You need to understand how Autodesk has already customized AutoCAD so that you don't inadvertently "step" on one of its features and make AutoCAD *less* productive rather than more productive. A lack of understanding of how this customization has been accomplished makes this a possible danger. You bought AutoCAD to increase your productivity. So why settle for anything less than the *most* you can get from your system?

However, increasing your productivity is more than learning how to change AutoCAD. It's optimizing AutoCAD's tools to help you work as efficiently as possible. And it involves understanding your operating environment so your projects run smoothly, without disasters. Productivity is your reward when you take AutoCAD's graphics engine to its limits and make it your CAD system.

How This Book Can Help

The real power of AutoCAD lies in the ease with which it can be customized to make your work simpler, not more complex. AutoCAD, designed to provide everything for everybody, is complex enough by its very nature. But you don't need to use *all* those options *all* the time. You should make the CAD system do it your way.

Over the last several years, AutoCAD has changed dramatically. It can not only *do* more; it's also now possible to run AutoCAD on a wide range of operating systems, platforms and environments. It's important to us at Ventana Press that our readers have the most up-to-date information possible to effectively work with AutoCAD, regardless of what system they're using.

This Sixth Edition of the *AutoCAD Productivity Book* is designed specifically to work with AutoCAD Releases 13 for Windows/NT, but most of what's here is equally applicable to other platforms.

To help you become more efficient, the *AutoCAD Productivity Book* gives you practical hands-on exercises, not just page after page of theory. Here are a few of the things you'll learn how to do:

- Control regenerations.
- Use multiple selection sets.
- Make the display list work for you.
- Work with all the menus.
- Create and customize dialog boxes.
- Make one menu control the others.
- Avoid pitfalls when working with menus.
- Make your own image tile menus.
- Learn to customize your own toolbars.
- Make your own hatch patterns and linetypes.
- Organize and protect your drawings, and handle any problems that arise.

You'll find that following the step-by-step instructions in these chapters is the best way to understand and master the concepts you need to make AutoCAD *your* CAD system.

What's Inside

The *AutoCAD Productivity Book* is organized into 14 tutorial chapters, an additional chapter featuring 30 ready-to-run programs and macros and three useful appendices that focus on specific information.

By using these programs and macros, you'll benefit from the enhancements at the same time you're learning what makes them work. And you'll quickly learn how much time and money they'll save you. (For an even faster start, use the *AutoCAD Productivity Companion Disk* inside the back cover, containing all the programs in this book.)

Prerequisites

AutoCAD/AutoLISP

This book is aimed at the user with nothing more than a basic knowledge of AutoCAD; you needn't be a CAD expert. If you can load AutoCAD, use a DOS or Windows editor, produce some lines, circles and arcs and save the drawing, you have the prerequisites to begin learning how to be more productive.

You don't need to know AutoLISP to use this book (although learning AutoLISP is, in fact, one of the most productive achievements you aim for). The AutoLISP used here is either self-contained in the ready-to-run programs or, when necessary, taught by example in the course of the discussion at hand. And Appendix B, "Using AutoLISP," provides everything you need to know in order to load and run the programs.

If you don't know AutoLISP and want to learn it, read *AutoLISP in Plain English* (Ventana Press). You'll be glad you did.

Software & Hardware Requirements

Although systems vary enormously, here's a brief rundown of a basic system assumed by this book.

- Release 13 of AutoCAD.
- Any computer system capable of running AutoCAD.
- Mouse or digitizer.
- Text editor. EDIT, Windows Write, Windows Notepad or even Edlin. (Appendix A discusses how to use text editors effectively.) Or you can use any other text editor or word processor you're familiar with.

How to Use This Book

The *AutoCAD Productivity Book* is a learning book, not a reference guide. Keep it in front of you as you use your computer. You'll really begin to learn what is being taught only when you see it happen on your own computer.

To make sure we're all speaking the same language, the items below define the conventions and procedures used in the book.

Type: Whenever you see this word in the page margins, type exactly what's shown, including all brackets, parentheses, forward and backward slashes, colons, semicolons, commas, spaces, etc. Exceptions would be key names, such as Enter, Alt, Ctrl or function keys (F1, F2, etc.).

<Enter> Press the Return or Enter key. This is also the same thing as a carriage return.

Press: This instructs you to choose a specific command or option from a menu, or press the command or function keys or buttons on a dialog box.

Response: This gives you the computer's response as it appears on the screen. This may be only a close approximation, due to differences among software versions, platforms and/or operating environments.

The AutoCAD Online Companion

Appendix C contains complete information about the *AutoCAD Online Companion*, a valuable AutoCAD resource maintained by the Ventana Online Internet site. Be sure to check out the online companion for all the latest AutoCAD information available. You'll also find archives of Auto-CAD programs and utilities, as well as links to other AutoCAD-related resources on the Net.

You're on Your Way . . .

. . . to becoming even more productive with AutoCAD than you ever thought possible. There's a lot in the *AutoCAD Productivity Book*. Take it one step at a time, and you'll see results from the very first chapter. Invest in productivity just as you've invested in AutoCAD, and the return will be an astounding surge in performance.

1

How Choices Affect Productivity

How Choices Affect Productivity

AutoCAD is a rich and complex program. For beginners, AutoCAD's complexity can seem overwhelming. AutoCAD's competitors try to use this to their advantage by promoting their programs as less complex and therefore easier to learn. But they fail to mention that "easier to learn" doesn't necessarily translate into "easier to use."

Language is a funny thing. If I use the word "complex" to describe AutoCAD, you immediately think of "difficult." On the other hand, if I describe AutoCAD as "rich in features and options," your interpretation is entirely different.

Both descriptions are accurate, however. AutoCAD is rich because it gives you all the tools you need to do what you want to do. This is where AutoCAD's power lies. But AutoCAD also gives you choices. Depending on what you're doing, certain choices applied to one situation can make you more productive, while the same choices in another situation may not produce such positive results.

Therefore, it's more important to learn *why* something is useful and what its potential effect on your productivity will be rather than simply to learn *how* to do it. To illustrate, let's look at how some of your major choices can help or hinder productivity when you're setting up a drawing.

Regenerations

 You don't have to work with AutoCAD for long before you realize that you don't want to have anything to do with regenerations. They're slow, and they cost you time and productivity. Can you forever avoid them? Do you need regenerations?

What Is a Regeneration?

To understand regenerations, it's necessary to understand how an Auto-CAD drawing is put together. The AutoCAD drawing is a *vector* database. This means that AutoCAD describes an object as a "line" on a "layer" of a "color," with a beginning and ending XYZ coordinate. Unfortunately, you can't see a description like this for every object. Therefore, AutoCAD translates these vectors into *raster* images. A raster file tells your graphics card and monitor which pixel dot to light up and what color to make it. This translation process is a regeneration of the drawing.

Once the regeneration has taken place, the raster information is saved in a *display list*. When AutoCAD needs to refresh the screen, wouldn't it be faster to replay the display list than to rebuild it from the vector information? Of course it would. This is what a *redraw* is—a replay of the display list. A regeneration is a complete rebuilding of a display list from the vector information.

AutoCAD's vector format stores its information in floating point decimals, giving AutoCAD incredibly high precision. Unfortunately, mathematics that involves floating point decimals can take much longer than math using integers. So when AutoCAD builds its initial display list for the screen, it has to work with no more than 600 to 1,600 pixel dots (integer numbers) per line of pixels on the screen, depending on the resolution capability of your graphics card and monitor.

While AutoCAD is building this display list for the monitor, it's also building the *Virtual Screen*. (We'll see how this works shortly.)

Why Do You Need a Regeneration?

The simple answer is that if something isn't part of your display list, you can't see it on the screen. The only way to make raster information part of your display list is to perform at least one regeneration.

But there are other reasons for regenerations. For example, the information on how blocks and layers are displayed is stored in block and layer *table definitions*. (This is the area in which AutoCAD stores the objects that will be used in block inserts and the global information concerning layers.) The objects in the object vector database reference only information in the various table definitions. Therefore, any changes to table definitions, such as changes in the block or layer definitions, will require a regeneration of the drawing before they can be reflected in the visual display list.

Other reasons for regenerations relate to 3D activities. In fact, virtually anything you do in 3D has the potential of involving a regeneration at one time or another. Multiple viewports require different display lists, even though they work with the same database. Therefore, any viewport creation done with either the VPORTS or the MVIEW command (the Model Space viewports created in Paper Space) requires a regeneration—

and you can imagine how many representations there might be as you rotate a drawing's view with the DVIEW command.

Can you work in AutoCAD without regenerations? No, obviously. You need at least one regeneration when your drawing first appears in the drawing editor. But it's possible, with a little understanding and experience, to minimize the number of regenerations and thus avoid their nonproductive consequences.

The REGENAUTO Command

This is the most important command available for reducing the number of regenerations that AutoCAD performs. Its format and control are simple.

Type: `REGENAUTO <Enter>`

Response: `ON/OFF [On]:`

Type: `Off <Enter>`

Under many circumstances, AutoCAD decides that it's necessary to perform a regeneration. In such cases, you want to know in advance if AutoCAD is about to regenerate so you can stop it if necessary. Auto-CAD's REGENAUTO command lets you set automatic regenerations to Off or On. If REGENAUTO is set to Off, you'll be given the message "About to regen—proceed? <Y>" before the regeneration takes place. You should generally answer No to this question.

But the following commands automatically require a regeneration and do not give you the option of responding Yes or No:

- ZOOM ALL
- ZOOM EXTENTS
- REGEN
- VIEWRES
- DVIEW

There are still other commands that do not ask you whether you want to regenerate, but the effect of these commands doesn't take place until the next regeneration. If these commands are entered or you are working with a transparent command that will require a regeneration, AutoCAD gives you the following prompt: "Regen queued." This means that the regeneration has been suppressed so that you can complete the command. But AutoCAD has stored the fact that it needs a regeneration, so that if you turn REGENAUTO back on, the regeneration will take place. Of course if you need to see what the regeneration would have produced on the screen, you can always enter **REGEN** from the command line. Some of these commands and circumstances are as follows:

- Block redefinitions
- Changes in text styles
- LTSCALE
- QTEXT

So if you've set REGENAUTO to Off and a command doesn't display what you expected it to, chances are it's waiting for the next regeneration. If you turn REGENAUTO on after it has been off for a while, and a regeneration is needed at that point, AutoCAD will perform one regeneration.

Although these may be minor inconveniences, it's important that AutoCAD not regenerate inadvertently, especially during ZOOM commands. Unless your drawing is extremely small, and a regeneration doesn't matter in overall speed and productivity, it's recommended that REGENAUTO be turned off.

The Virtual Screen

Zooming has been one of the main reasons for regenerations in AutoCAD in the past. Over the years this has been such a problem that third-party developers have created graphics cards and programs to make certain you can zoom anywhere in your drawing without regenerating it.

AutoCAD product improvements have come a long way in eliminating this problem. One of these improvements is the Virtual Screen. And now with Release 13, AutoCAD has incorporated display list processing complete with an Aerial View window as a standard feature.

During a regeneration, AutoCAD not only builds the display list for the real screen, it also builds a greatly expanded Virtual Screen. The real screen's size may be between 600 and 1,600 integers, representing the pixel resolutions per line, while the Virtual Screen in Release 11 has over 32,000 pixels per line, still represented by integers. In Release 13, this has been expanded to more than 4 billion pixels! Therefore, if you follow a few simple rules, a regeneration caused by the ZOOM command should now be a thing of the past.

The real screen can display only a small portion of the drawing, depending on the zoomed-in area you're viewing. As you move around in your drawing, you may move out of your real-screen view. This is where the Virtual Screen comes in: the real screen can pick up the additional pixel images it needs by translating from the larger Virtual Screen. Because the Virtual Screen and the real screen both are described using integers, the translation is much faster from the Virtual Screen than from the vector database during a regeneration.

The key, then, is to be sure that as you move around in the drawing, you stay inside the Virtual Screen. As long as you do this, and the zoomed-in area or magnification can be displayed from the pixel information in the Virtual Screen, AutoCAD will use REDRAW or at least a display translation in integer form rather than REGEN.

If you ZOOM, PAN or request a restored view that either is outside the Virtual Screen or specifies a magnification that's impossible to accomplish, a regeneration will occur. What's worse, the regeneration will reestablish the new area as the new Virtual Screen. This is all right if that's what you want; but generally you'll need another regeneration to get back to where you were.

Respect for the Virtual Screen can mean the difference in whether you use REGEN or REDRAW while zooming. If you ever move out of the Virtual Screen, AutoCAD will regenerate. How do you know where the Virtual Screen is? Well, under ordinary circumstances you can't see where it is, but you can make the area of the Virtual Screen visible by entering **ZOOM V**. When you do this, your drawing will move to the center of the screen and it will be surrounded by a large empty area. The edge of this empty space on your screen is the boundary of the Virtual Screen.

In Release 11, the ZOOM V command could actually be used as a substitute for ZOOM ALL. It should not be used this way in Releases 12 and 13, however, because the large maximum area of the Virtual Screen will generally show only a small portion of your real drawing.

What Is the VIEWRES Command?

The VIEWRES command turns the Virtual Screen on or off. If the area you're working in is small enough, it's possible that the creation of a Virtual Screen can slow AutoCAD down. If your work area fits nicely in your real screen's 1,000 pixels per line, you may want to turn off the

Virtual Screen with the VIEWRES command. But rarely would I recommend turning off VIEWRES.

The first question that VIEWRES asks is, "Do you want fast zooms? <Y>." This is a silly question. No one will say, "No, I want slow zooms—in fact, make them *really* slow." The question should be "Do you want AutoCAD to create a Virtual Screen?" But if you answer No to this question, all ZOOMs, PANs and VIEW RESTOREs will regenerate.

The next question is a little more confusing. VIEWRES asks you to

```
Enter circle zoom percent (1-20000) <100>:
```

The purpose of this information is to optimize AutoCAD's speed in redrawing circles, arcs and linetypes. If you have no (or few) circles, arcs or special linetypes, the redraw will be about the same, no matter what you set as VIEWRES percent of circle. On the other hand, if there are many circles or arcs in a drawing, you can save calculation time at REDRAW if you use a low number for VIEWRES percent.

AutoCAD defaults to a value of 100 for VIEWRES percent. This tells AutoCAD to use its internal algorithm without alteration. Therefore, when you zoom in on a circle, it will display the circle or arc using straight line segments. The higher you raise the VIEWRES percent, the smoother the circles and arcs are as you zoom. If you change the VIEWRES percent to 2000, you can zoom in by up to a factor of 20 and still have smooth circles and arcs.

Unless your drawing is made up largely of arcs and circles, to the point that VIEWRES percent makes a difference, try using 2000 instead of 100 to improve your productivity. If you use 100, circles and arcs, as mentioned, will be made up of straight line segments. This can be an occasional problem if you need the drawing properly displayed. You can always force a regeneration—the circles and arcs will be smoothed. You only have to do this once to make up for any minor savings that VIEWRES 100 may give you. This is how VIEWRES can be changed:

Type: `VIEWRES <Enter>`

Response: `Do you want fast Zooms? <Y>`

Type: `Y <Enter>`

If you answer No to this question, a Virtual Screen will not be created and you will regenerate every time you ZOOM.

Response: `Percentage of Circle <100>`

The default is 100 if you're running AutoCAD straight out of the box. (This should not be considered the recommended value.) Otherwise, the default is the last setting made.

Type: `2000 <Enter>`

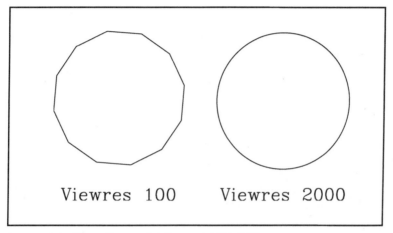

Figure 1-1: The effects of different VIEWRES percents.

The LIMITS Command

The LIMITS command sets up boundaries around your drawing area. Although you're not required to set limits, there are several reasons why you should do so before you begin working in an AutoCAD drawing.

Most drawings must eventually be plotted at a given scale on a given size sheet of paper. Setting limits keeps your drawing within the size and scale you've selected. One of the best reasons for using limits is that it makes plotting simple. If the limits are set to the effective drawing area of your paper in Model Space, then plotting by limits is the easiest and most accurate method of plotting. Even if you're using Paper Space, the limits set to the effective drawing area of the paper when plotted at 1:1 will assure that the accurate coordinates are being plotted. When you set limits, you can also use the GRID command, which allows you to see the limits. If you don't work within set limits, the grid is not available to you.

LIMITS lets you use system variables such as LIMMIN and LIMMAX in AutoLISP programs to set scales or for other purposes. If you use the system variable LIMCHECK or the On subcommand of LIMITS, Auto-CAD will make sure you're not drawing outside the drawing limits. This works to some degree but isn't infallible. For example, a circle that begins within the limits may eventually exceed the limits, without giving you an "Outside Limits" error message.

LIMITS also controls the area defined by ZOOM ALL, as long as there are no objects outside the limits.

Prototype Drawings

In addition to what we've covered so far, there are many other specifications that can be set up so they'll be there when your new drawing begins. They include blocks, layers, text styles, dimension variables—the list goes on. You can place all these settings in a prototype drawing.

You're allowed one prototype drawing by default, but you may have as many as you need. If you're using AutoCAD out of the box, the name of your default prototype drawing is ACAD.DWG. This means that when a new drawing is created, it will use a copy of ACAD.DWG as the new beginning drawing.

You can find out the name of your default prototype drawing, or change the name of your prototype drawing, by entering the configuration routine.

Choose Configure from the Options pull-down menu.

Type: <Enter>

This gets you past the configuration description and takes you to the Configuration menu. (You may have to press Enter several times to get past your current configuration description.)

Type: 7 <Enter>

Response: (AutoCAD responds with the operating parameters menu.)

Type: 2 <Enter>

Response: Enter name of default prototype file for new drawings or . for none <ACAD.DWG>.

AutoCAD responds with the name of your default prototype drawing. At this point, you may change it or press Enter to leave it as is.

Type: 0 <Enter> (This returns you to the Configuration menu.)

Type: 0 <Enter>

Response: (AutoCAD asks if you want to save the configuration changes.)

Type: Y <Enter>

You're now returned to the AutoCAD drawing editor. When you begin a new drawing, you're really beginning with a copy of your default prototype drawing as defined in the previous configuration file. Therefore, once the prototype drawing is properly set up, all new drawings will begin properly set up.

Selecting a Prototype Drawing

The procedure for using prototype drawings differs from release to release. The following is the procedure for selecting any prototype drawing with Release 13 even though it is not your default prototype. When you create a new drawing, you'll be given a dialog box within which to give the new drawing a name (see Figure 1-2).

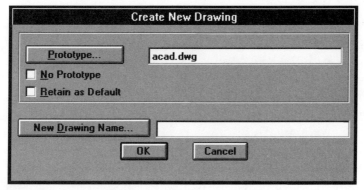

Figure 1-2: Create New Drawing dialog box with Prototype button.

Pick Prototype from the dialog box. This activates a Prototype Drawing File dialog box (see Figure 1-3), defaulting to the drive and directory of your current prototype drawing, which is named in the box to the right of Prototype. Use the dialog box to find and pick the prototype you want to use.

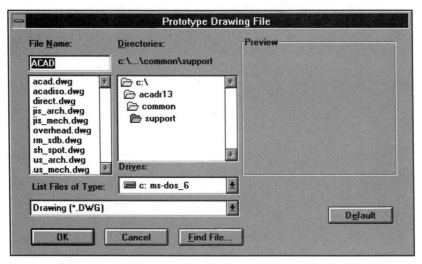

Figure 1-3: Prototype Drawing File dialog box.

Release 13 gives you an easy way to create and access a whole library of prototype drawings. In a library, similar things are usually in the same place. In AutoCAD versions before Release 12, this principle didn't seem to apply to prototype drawings. For instance, in Release 10 or 11, when you used the command NEWDWG=PROTODWG, AutoCAD couldn't find your prototype drawing unless it was your default prototype or you gave it the drive path specifications.

This is not the case with Releases 12 and 13. You can keep an entire library of prototype drawings in a single directory. Let's assume you call it C:\DWG\PROTO. Place all your prototype drawings in this directory.

You must now tell AutoCAD not only where to find your prototype drawings but also which one is to be your default prototype drawing. To do this, begin a new drawing. You are given a Create New Drawing dialog box. Pick Prototype. This brings up a Prototype Drawing File dialog box. Click in the Directories box until you have selected the \DWG\PROTO directory. This changes the default directory to C:\DWG\PROTO. Now select in the File Name list the drawing you want to use as your prototype. Select OK. This returns you to the Create New Drawing dialog box. Now pick the Retain as Default check box. You can give the new drawing a name, but it's not necessary. What matters this first time is that you OK the dialog box.

You've just created a default prototype drawing. This can be ACAD.DWG or any other drawing you want to use as the default prototype. It's important that you also tell AutoCAD where to find all your prototype drawings (as long as the default prototype drawing is in the same directory as the others). From now on, you can choose any prototype drawing merely by picking Prototype and then picking the drawing. The default directory will contain your prototype drawing library.

Remember—any drawing can be the default if you pick the Retain as Default check box before you OK the Create New Drawing dialog box.

Moving On

Setting up your drawings properly is the first step in improving your productivity with AutoCAD. Of course, AutoCAD will be productive for you no matter what you do or how you do it. But it's possible to do things a better way. Our goal is to achieve the highest possible productivity from AutoCAD. We want to take it to its limits. And on that point, in Chapter 2 you'll see that the unprecedented enhancements built into Release 13 push AutoCAD's capabilities well beyond any limits ever imagined.

2

The New
Release 13
for Windows

The New Release 13 for Windows

Release 13 is a dramatic departure from other AutoCAD releases, and not just because of its many new features. After all, every new release has new features. The real difference lies in the tools that are built in so users and third-party developers can add features to AutoCAD.

Release 13, with licenses for both Windows and DOS, is the first AutoCAD version in years in which the core program has been rewritten. The changes made to the core architecture will permit Autodesk and other developers to work with the product in a modular manner for many years to come. AutoCAD has been completely redesigned, but the changes are totally transparent to the user.

In this chapter you're going to learn how AutoCAD is put together and where to find what you need. After all, there is so much information in the AutoCAD reference guides, where do you look first? You'll learn what happens after you select the ACADR13 icon. There's a lot going on behind the scenes when you bring up a new drawing. If you change something without knowing what you're doing, many of those new features won't work for you.

You'll also see how your own AutoLISP programs can be added to AutoCAD and made to function like many of Release 13's new features. Finally, you'll learn about dialog boxes and how they fit into the overall new productivity potential of Release 13. (In Chapter 14, there's a practical tutorial on creating your own dialog boxes.)

Let's begin by seeing how Autodesk has used its own tools to customize AutoCAD for you in Release 13.

Customizing by the Book

AutoCAD's Release 13 comes packaged with three main manuals. Begin your acquaintance with Release 13 by thumbing through them. The *User's Guide* covers everything you need to know about the AutoCAD core program. This is a complete reference manual, not a tutorial intended to teach you AutoCAD (although you can learn a lot by reading it). The *Command Reference Guide* is an alphabetical explanation of all of the AutoCAD commands. This manual has been long overdue. The *Customization Guide* contains the information you need for ADS, AutoLISP and dialog boxes.

Most of the dialog boxes in Release 13 are in the form of AutoLISP programs that run the .DCL files and other programs such as ADS programs. There are some programs that in previous versions were BONUS programs. These earlier programs were difficult to use because they required some basic AutoLISP knowledge to load and run. But Release 13 has added all these programs to AutoCAD's basic menu structure. So now, you simply choose them from the existing menu system, and they're loaded and executed as transparently as any core AutoCAD command. In fact, they can be used interchangeably with core AutoCAD commands.

Customizing AutoCAD requires a thorough understanding of AutoLISP. The *Customization Guide* is a technical reference manual; it's not intended to teach AutoLISP to nonprogrammers. If you want to learn AutoLISP, read *AutoLISP in Plain English* (published by Ventana Press). The *Customization Guide* is not a beginner's book. It does not try to teach you how or why you should customize AutoCAD. That's the subject of *this* book. The *AutoCAD Customization Guide* is a reference manual for some of the customization tools you'll be using. It goes into more detail and explores more advanced concepts for professionals than are presented here.

Menus & AutoLISP Files

Let's take a look at how Release 13 has been customized. When you start AutoCAD Release 13 "out of the box," it begins by loading the last—or default—template menu file. This is generally the ACAD.MNU file. (As you'll learn, it actually doesn't load the .MNU file directly, but instead loads the compiled .MNC file by the same name—ACAD.MNC.) It also loads the ACAD.MNT and the ACAD.MNR files. Then you'll see the statement "AutoCAD Release 13 menu utilities loaded."

There's a lot going on behind these simple words. In Release 11, the ACAD.MNU file was getting too big to handle, mainly because there were scores of embedded AutoLISP programs in the menu structure itself. For the most part, all AutoLISP programs have now been removed from the Release 13 menu. It's now a much simpler and cleaner menu. But a new file structure—the .MNL file—has been created.

The .MNL file is a companion AutoLISP file to the .MNU file. Therefore, there is a matching ACAD.MNL file for ACAD.MNU. (The .MNL file must carry the same name as the corresponding .MNU file.) But don't jump to conclusions: commands in the .MNU file don't actually access the .MNL file, which is like an additional ACAD.LSP file. Think of .MNU as "menu" and .MNL as "menu: LISP."

In AutoLISP, the ACAD.LSP file is loaded automatically each time a new or existing drawing is begun in the drawing editor. The problem is that only one ACAD.LSP file can be loaded automatically. Programmers have tried all kinds of tricks to get around this. Generally, they've had the ACAD.LSP file load other files, but that didn't necessarily tie the various .LSP files to a given menu structure. Now you can have an infinite number of automatically loaded AutoLISP files that are loaded only when the appropriate menu is loaded. That's what an .MNL file really is: an Auto-LISP file that's loaded when its corresponding menu file is loaded. That way, you're assured that any AutoLISP commands you might use are already loaded when the menu is changed. The concept of an .MNL file is not limited to the base or template menu file. As you will learn, AutoCAD has the ability to use loadable menus that are added to the menu bar. These can be your own loadable menus or loadable menus provided to you by third-party developers. Each of these loadable .MNU files may have a corresponding .MNL file as well.

If you type out the ACAD.MNL file found in the SUPPORT directory, you'll see the following line toward the beginning of the file, after the copyright notice:

```
(princ "\nAutoCAD Release 13 menu utilities ")
```

The statement on the command line at the beginning of each drawing comes from this ACAD.MNL file. Please note that, depending on how you install AutoCAD (e.g., Windows only, DOS only or Windows and DOS), three major directories under ACADR13 may be created. They are \ACADR13\COMMON, \ACADR13\DOS and \ACADR13\WIN. Within each of these directories is a subdirectory called SUPPORT. The files that are specific to DOS are in the \ACADR13\DOS\SUPPORT directory. The files specific to Windows are located in the \ACADR13\WIN\SUPPORT directory. And the files that will work with both DOS and Windows are in the \ACADR13\COMMON\SUPPORT directory. Throughout the book this will be referred to as the SUPPORT directory. Depending on how your AutoCAD is installed, you may have to check to see which of the support directories contains the file.

So what do Release 13 menu utilities do? They provide essential operations to the ACAD.MNU file; and one of the most important is the loading of an AutoLISP file known as ACADR13.LSP.

Some of the real AutoLISP code resides in the ACADR13.LSP file, but even this file is relatively small. It contains utility programs used by other programs. It also sets certain system variables. One of its main programs is an ingenious AutoLISP program known as AUTOLOAD. This file also contains the names of the programs, especially the dialog box programs, that are eligible to be loaded. Let's look at a portion of the AUTOLOAD routine found in the ACADR13.LSP file.

```
;;;===== AutoLoad LISP Applications =====
(autoload "appload" '("appload" "appload"))
(autoload "edge"   '("edge"))
(autoload "filter" '("filter " "filter"))
(autoload "3d" '("3d" "3d" "ai_box" "ai_pyramid" "ai_wedge" "ai_dome"
                 "ai_mesh" "ai_sphere" "ai_cone" "ai_torus" "ai_dish"))
(autoload "ddinsert" '("ddinsert"))
(autoload "ddattdef" '("ddattdef"))
(autoload "ddattext" '("ddattext"))
(autoload "3darray" '("3darray"))
(autoload "ddmodify" '("ddmodify"))
(autoload "ddchprop" '("ddchprop"))
(autoload "ddview" '("ddview"))
(autoload "ddvpoint" '("ddvpoint"))
(autoload "mvsetup" '("mvsetup"))
(autoload "ddosnap" '("ddosnap"))
(autoload "ddptype" '("ddptype"))
(autoload "dducsp" '("dducsp"))
(autoload "ddunits" '("ddunits"))
(autoload "ddgrips" '("ddgrips"))
(autoload "ddselect" '("ddselect"))
(autoload "ddrename" '("ddrename"))
(autoload "ddcolor" '("ddcolor"))
(autoload "xrefclip" '("xrefclip"))
(autoload "attredef" '("attredef"))
(autoload "xplode" '("xp" "xplode"))
```

Remember that this is only one part of the overall AUTOLOAD system of programs—but one that you can use immediately. For example, the last entry is an AutoLISP program called XPLODE. It will be loaded the first time you issue the XPLODE command, either by typing it in or choosing it through a menu system.

At first glance, it almost looks like magic. Nowhere in this file is there any mention of loading the XPLODE.LSP file. Then how does the file get loaded? Without getting bogged down in the complex code the Autodesk programmers use, let's take a simplistic example.

Let's assume you had the following lines in a traditional ACAD.LSP file:

```
(defun C:xplode ()
  (load "xplode")
  (C:xplode)
)
```

You would now have a loaded AutoLISP function called XPLODE. But this function is not the real XPLODE program—it's only a function by the same name that first loads XPLODE.LSP, then executes the newly loaded XPLODE function. In this way, you don't have to load the entire file at all times; you need only enough code to load the larger file any time the name of the file or command is executed.

Why couldn't you just include the traditional "if not" AutoLISP statement in the menu? You could, but that wouldn't load the file if the command were typed in instead of being accessed from the menu. This method loads the file regardless of how it is entered.

To repeat, this is a simplistic explanation, although the above code actually works with any version of AutoCAD. The actual AUTOLOAD program has many error-checking features and provides a simple way of including your favorite AutoLISP programs without knowing a lot about AutoLISP.

Let's look at the syntax of the code that loads and executes the XPLODE command:

```
(autoload "xplode" '("xp" "xplode"))
```

The code begins as an AutoLISP function with *(autoload*. This is followed by the name of the actual file to be loaded (in quotes)—*"xplode"*. Do not add .LSP to the file name. The next group—*'("xplode" "xp"))*—gets a little tricky. In AutoLISP, the apostrophe (') means to treat the next group of items as a list. Therefore, '("xplode" "xp") is a list of names you can use for the command. In this case, you could type either **xplode** or **xp** at the command line to execute the XPLODE command. You can have as many names (or aliases) for a command as you want. Begin the series with '(then list the names in quotations, separated by a space. Close the list with a). Finally, the entire function ends in a).

Let's use an example from this book. Say you want to add the LISP "Break Text" program (from Chapter 15, "The AutoCAD Productivity Library") to a group of programs that would be loaded automatically. Also assume you want to be able to access the program by either of two names, BRKTXT or the alias BT.

On the *AutoCAD Productivity Companion Disk* in the back of this book, you'll find the program in the file BRKTXT.LSP. Copy the file to the ACADR13\WIN\SUPPORT directory. If you create the file from scratch, create it as BRKTXT.LSP and locate it in the SUPPORT directory. To make it load automatically, you'll now need to edit the ACADR13.LSP file.

Caution! Before modifying any existing AutoCAD files, be sure to back up those files. In fact, you may want to copy the entire SUPPORT directory to another temporary directory where it will be safe. If necessary, you can restore the files from the temporary directory.

The following example will ask you to search for a section of text within a text file such as the ACADR13.LSP file. This example assumes that the file is loaded into a text editor. For DOS this might be EDIT.EXE and for Windows it can be the Notepad program. These programs and other text editors have search capabilities that permit you to search for specific strings of text and bring you to the first occurrence of that text when it is found.

In the ACADR13.LSP file, search for the following:

```
;;;===== AutoLoad LISP Applications =====
```

In this section of the file, enter the following on a line by itself:

```
(autoload "brktxt" '("brktxt" "bt"))
```

Now save the ACADR13.LSP file.

Notice that you've permitted the program to be accessed by either brktxt or bt. But there is no command function or alias called BT in the program file. If you're satisfied with only using brktxt to bring up the program, then the (autoload functions should simply read as follows:

```
(autoload "brktxt" '("brktxt"))
```

If you also want to be able to use an alias of bt as the name of the program, you'll have to add one line to the BRKTXT.LSP file you placed in the SUPPORT directory. Go to the end of the BRKTXT.LSP file and add the following statement:

```
(defun C:bt () (C:brktxt))
```

This is a new function, called C:bt, that starts the C:brktxt function. You would need to add a statement similar to this at the end of each AutoLISP file in which you'll access the same program by several different names.

Begin a new drawing or start an existing drawing. All you have to do to start the program is enter **bt** or **brktxt**, and the program will begin. See how easy it is? This gives you a convenient way to add your favorite AutoLISP programs to Release 13.

Dialog Boxes

Dialog boxes provide an interactive environment a level above menu and icon customization or even traditional AutoLISP programs. You're insulated from the actual workings of the program and you're not restricted to a series of ordered choices. You choose the order in which you'll interact with the dialog box.

The most visible change in Release 13 is the number of dialog boxes available; but the real advantage is the feature that allows you to create *programmable* dialog boxes through the .DCL language.

You'll find a tutorial on constructing dialog boxes in Chapter 14. For now, suffice it to say that most dialog boxes are a combination of two files: one file contains the description of the dialog box layout (found in the SUPPORT directory with the .DCL file extension); the companion file is a regular AutoLISP file of the same name as the .DCL file. The AutoLISP file activates and runs the dialog box. It not only activates the dialog box and brings it to the screen but also controls what happens when one of the options in the dialog box is chosen.

Let's take a look at the DDRENAME command and trace it to see how it's put together. First, there are two files in the SUPPORT directory. DDRENAME.LSP runs the program and calls up the dialog box, and DDRENAME.DCL describes the dialog box layout on the screen and the various buttons and scroll boxes available. How does AutoCAD know anything about DDRENAME as a command? It knows the same things about this command as it does any other AutoLISP command.

```
(autoload "ddrename" '("ddrename"))
```

Autodesk placed the above statement in the ACADR13.LSP file with other AUTOLOAD commands. Therefore, when **ddrename** was entered at the command line or picked from a menu, AUTOLOAD loaded and executed the AutoLISP program. The AutoLISP program began and controlled the dialog box.

Toolbars

One of the most interesting new features of Release 13 is the addition of toolbars. (This feature is not available in the DOS version.) Their creation and modification will be discussed in Chapter 9, but for now note that the definition of the toolbars is stored in the menu file. From the .MNU file AutoCAD automatically creates an .MNS file. AutoCAD places the toolbar definition in the ***TOOLBARS section of this file. Any time the toolbars are changed, the .MNS file is also modified and saved. In the Windows version the .MNS file is compiled to the .MNC file. This is the actual file that is loaded.

Moving On

Are you beginning to see how neatly everything fits into place? Rarely do you hear mentioned the big new feature of Release 13: the various interfaces embedded in the core program that allow true customization. This change opens up exciting possibilities for the future. The best new features of future releases will be external programs. This means that an explosion of new features for AutoCAD can be brought to market by Autodesk, as well as by third-party vendors, without touching the basic core program.

The chapters that follow provide you with the basic tools you'll need to increase your own productivity and the know-how to master the coming explosion of competing packages and enhancements for AutoCAD. Chapter 3 introduces the fundamentals of the basic menu construction. Let's get started…

3

Menus & How They Work

Menus & How They Work

As AutoCAD has evolved, its menu structure has become more and more complex. But that doesn't mean it's difficult to learn—if you master the rules. Once you understand how the menu structure works, you're well on your way to increasing your productivity.

First, let's look at what a menu file is. There are two major types of menu files: .MNU and .MNS files. The .MNU file, the one you will be most comfortable with, will work in both Windows and DOS. If you create your menus with an .MNU file, Windows will automatically create the corresponding .MNS file for you. For now, we'll discuss only the .MNU file.

The .MNU file is the main template file for any menu you create, including the AutoCAD main menu (ACAD.MNU) and any other menus created by you or a third-party developer.

In DOS, AutoCAD automatically compiles the .MNU file to an .MNX file. In Windows, AutoCAD first creates or modifies the .MNS file from the .MNU file and then compiles the .MNS file to an .MNC file. This procedure occurs any time a change is made in the .MNU file. (An .MNX, .MNC or .MNS file carries the same name as its corresponding .MNU file.) Therefore, you really don't have to worry about compiling the .MNX or the .MNC file. AutoCAD, recognizing when a change has been made in the template menu's source code, automatically compiles and executes the .MNX or .MNC file when you enter the drawing editor or when the menu is called up. But it's a good idea to check periodically to be sure that the .MNX or .MNC file is compiling when necessary. (More on that later.)

Additional menu files used in Windows include .MNR files (Windows resource files, which contain bitmaps used by menus) and .MND files (menu definition files containing macros). An .MNL is an automatic loading AutoLISP file that loads with the menu of the same name.

In the drawing editor you'll see that AutoCAD uses a number of different types of menus: the screen menu, pull-down, cursor, image, plus button and tablet menus. In Windows you have additional features including toolbars, keyboard accelerators, help strings and tooltips.

Working With ACAD.MNU

As mentioned before, the ACAD.MNU file is the main AutoCAD template menu—the menu that's supplied to you straight out of the box. Let's look at how the ACAD.MNU file is organized. Depending on the AutoCAD platform you're using, it's found in one of several different places. In the Windows version it is generally in the \ACADR13\WIN\SUPPORT directory.

Using a Text Editor

Since the ACAD.MNU template file is a text file, you'll use an ASCII text editor to work with the file. If you're in a DOS environment, you can use either EDIT or Edlin (if you have an old copy of Edlin available). Examples in this book assume a working knowledge of EDIT. For smaller files you can use Notepad for Windows or Write for Windows. These programs may not be able to load larger files.

Using a Word Processor

What about word processors? Generally, you can use any word processing program, as long as you take some simple precautions. First, make sure the file can be saved as an ordinary text file. If your word processor doesn't have this capability, you can't use it. You can test this by saving a file, then entering **Type** and the file name from the DOS prompt. See if you can read the file.

Type: `Type <name of file> <Enter>`

If you can read the file and it contains no extra or strange marks, then you've saved the file in a text format.

There's another precaution you must be aware of: make certain your margins are set for more than 80 characters. This is difficult to do with some advanced word processors. For example, Word for Windows and most other Windows word processing programs control the margins by intelligently looking at your printer and font setup. If your setup can't accommodate more than 80 characters to a line, setting the margins at 0 to the left and 0 to the right will do no good. Why? Here's what will happen.

The ACAD.MNU file has lines that are longer than your word processor will permit on a single line. If this occurs, the line will wrap around. If the file is saved this way the menu will become corrupted. To avoid this, try setting Windows up with a Generic/Text Only printer. Make this printer the default printer when working on AutoCAD files. Then set your margins 0 to the left and 0 from the right or as close to the edge as possible. This should give you enough room to keep the lines from word-wrapping. Another possibility is to reduce the size of the font. This should give you enough space to avoid word-wrapping.

Back Up Your Menu Often

Customizing a menu is an evolutionary process. If the menu is totally ruined, it's easier to start from a backup copy of the latest menu version than to try fixing it. Don't worry about destroying your menu file; if worse comes to worst, you can start from the ACAD.MNU file on your original disks.

Important: Make a copy in a separate directory of *.MN* now. If you mess up while working with this book, you will always have a way to get your original menus back. In fact, while you're learning it's a good idea to back up the entire SUPPORT directory. *Do it now!*

Take a Look at ACAD.MNU

Now it's time to take a look at the ACAD.MNU file. Use whatever text editor you wish and bring up the ACAD.MNU file. It is found in the SUPPORT directory. The first page of the file should appear on your screen and look similar to the following. But remember, in each platform (DOS or Windows) the file will be slightly different.

```
//      ACAD.MNU Version 13.0 for Release 13 Windows/NT
//
//      Copyright (C) 1986, 1987, 1988, 1989, 1990, 1991, 1992, 1994
//      by Autodesk, Inc.
//
//      Permission to use, copy, modify, and distribute this software
//      for any purpose and without fee is hereby granted, provided
//      that the above copyright notice appears in all copies and
//      that both that copyright notice and the limited warranty and
//      restricted rights notice below appear in all supporting
//      documentation.
//
//      AUTODESK PROVIDES THIS PROGRAM "AS IS" AND WITH ALL FAULTS.
//      AUTODESK SPECIFICALLY DISCLAIMS ANY IMPLIED WARRANTY OF
```

```
//       MERCHANTABILITY OR FITNESS FOR A PARTICULAR USE. AUTODESK, INC.
//       DOES NOT WARRANT THAT THE OPERATION OF THE PROGRAM WILL BE
//       UNINTERRUPTED OR ERROR FREE.
//
//       Use, duplication, or disclosure by the U.S. Government is subject to
//       restrictions set forth in FAR 52.227-19 (Commercial Computer
//       Software - Restricted Rights) and DFAR 252.227-7013(c)(1)(ii)
//       (Rights in Technical Data and Computer Software), as applicable.
//
//       Input to menu compiler mc(.exe) for acad.mnu.  See mc.doc.
//
//       NOTE:  AutoCAD looks for an ".mnl" (Menu Lisp) file whose name is
//              the same as that of the menu file, and loads it if
//              found.  If you modify this menu and change its name, you
//              should copy acad.mnl to <yourname>.mnl, since the menu
//              relies on AutoLISP routines found there.
//
//
//       Macro definition(s) to be expanded by mc(.exe):
//


//
//       Default AutoCAD Release 13 NAMESPACE declaration:
//

***MENUGROUP=ACAD

//
//    Begin AutoCAD Button Menus
//

***BUTTONS1
;
$p0=*
```

```
^C^C
^B
^O
^G
^D
^E
^T


***BUTTONS2
$p0=*


***BUTTONS3
^c^cline


***AUX1
;
$p0=*
^C^C
^B
^O
^G
^D
^E
^T


***AUX2
$p0=*


***AUX3
^c^cline



//
//    Begin AutoCAD Pull-down Menus
//
```

Major Menu Areas

The AutoCAD menu system uses 10 major areas, shown in the following table.

ACAD.MNU Section	Description
MENUGROUP	Designates the name of menu groups
BUTTONS	Digitizer button section
AUX	Mouse button section
POP	Pull-down menus
IMAGE	Image tile section
SCREEN	Screen section
TABLET	Tablet section
ACCELERATORS	Keyboard shortcut keys
TOOLBARS	Toolbar definitions
HELPSTRINGS	Extended help string information

There are variations to each and suffixes to several of these areas. For example, you can have ***BUTTONS1 and ***BUTTONS2; ***POP1 and ***POP2; ***TABLET1 and ***TABLET2; and ***AUX1 and ***AUX2 sections. There are suffixes for alternate menus, too, such as ***TABLET1ALT. But for now, let's stay with the basics and let the finer details come into focus later.

Each major section serves a specific purpose. A major section must begin with three asterisks (***). The keyword following the asterisks is not user-definable. It's a keyword designated by AutoCAD. There are user-definable sections, as you'll see later, but user-definable sections can't begin with three asterisks.

***BUTTONS1 controls the buttons on your digitizer puck and ***AUX1 controls the buttons on your mouse. As a general practice, any time you modify the ***BUTTONS section, you should make the same change on the ***AUX section and vice versa. Here we will only talk about the ***AUX section to save space, but you should make corresponding changes to the ***BUTTONS counterpart as applicable or the button assignments won't work. We are assuming that you are using the default Windows pointing device. Each line represents a button on your mouse, as follows:

```
***AUX1
;
$p0=*
^C^C
^B
^0
^G
^D
^E
^THE
```

The first line following ***AUX1 represents the next button after your Pick button. You can't control the Pick button. Assume the Pick button is Button 1. Then, the semicolon (;) is the AutoCAD macro for Enter and is assigned to Button 2. Don't worry about what $p0=* means at this point. It's assigned to Button 3, ^C^C to Button 4, etc. You can continue this scenario for as many buttons as your mouse supports.

The ***POP sections represent your pull-down menus. The pull-down menus are numbered from left to right. The menus are designated ***POP1, ***POP2, ***POP3, etc. In Release 13, ***POP0 is reserved for the cursor menu. This is a special pull-down menu that is activated at the cursor crosshairs, not at the menu bar.

The ***SCREEN section represents the side screen menu system. The ***SCREEN section itself represents the beginning AutoCAD screen menu. Most of the screen menus are in user-definable sections.

The ***TABLET menus represent the four major tablet menu sections of your digitizer. Typically, these are defined using the TABLET CFG command in AutoCAD. Like the ***POP sections, the tablet menu sections are numbered: ***TABLET1, ***TABLET2, ***TABLET3, ***TABLET4.

The ***IMAGE section is reserved for the menu icons. Since AutoCAD uses the word *icons* to denote the toolbar images, AutoCAD has changed the name of the menu icons to *image tiles*. This is the most complicated of the sections, but it can prove to be the most productive if used correctly.

Multiple Buttons Menus

AutoCAD Release 13 supports four ***BUTTONS or ***AUX menu sections. Not everyone has a 16-button mouse. Many who run AutoCAD use only a 2-button or 3-button mouse. The additional ***AUX sections provide enhanced mouse support in the following ways:

Menu Section	Mouse Action Supported
***AUX1	Pick the button.
***AUX2	Hold the Shift key down and pick the button.
***AUX3	Hold the Ctrl key down and pick the button.
***AUX4	Hold the Ctrl and Shift keys down and pick the button.

User-Defined Areas

The *** sections are defined by AutoCAD, but you can define your own sections. User-defined sections of the menu are marked with two asterisks instead of three. The screen sections are the most frequently used user-defined areas.

A user-defined section can be created almost anywhere in the menu structure. Open up some lines and begin. Assume you want to create a screen menu section called **SPDRAW1. The safest thing to do is to place your section before another ** section. This technique avoids accidentally placing your section in the middle of another section. Following the **SPDRAW1, place any AutoCAD commands you wish. For example,

```
**SPDRAW1 3
[LINE]^c^cLINE
[CIRCLE-D]^c^c(command "circle" pause "D" pause)
[ARC]^c^cARC
[Erase L]^c^c(command "erase" "L" "")
```

**SPDRAW1 is the name of our menu. (Notice that a 3 follows the name—more about this shortly.) The next line begins with [LINE]. Anything in brackets [ ] is what appears on the screen menu as a prompt. If you don't use the brackets, the first few words of the command will be the prompt. This is all right if the prompt and the command are one and the same (without the ^c^c in front of them). But it's generally a good idea to use the brackets, because they give you the most control.

The ^c^c assures that any command you're already in will be canceled. This sequence is formed using the ^ (the caret mark, accessed by Shift+6) and the C on your keyboard. Don't use the Ctrl key. (The reason you need two ^c's is that some commands, like DIM, can be completely canceled only by issuing two Ctrl+C's.) Next is the command you want issued. Notice that we've combined some AutoCAD and AutoLISP commands. (See Appendix B, "Using AutoLISP," for the basics of using the minimum amount of AutoLISP in your menu structure.)

Some third-party programs toggle the system variable MENUECHO off (set it to 1). If this occurs and you set your button to an Object Snap such as endp (endpoint) or int (intersection), you won't see which Object Snap you are using at the command line. But there may be a legitimate reason for turning MENUECHO off. Preceding your button with a ^P will cause it to be echoed at the command line even if MENUECHO is set to 1. Be aware that if MENUECHO is set to 4, the ^P will not work. The following line in your ***AUX section will properly echo the endpoint and intersection:

```
^Pendp,int
```

If you're customizing menus for your own use, the following is only a curiosity, but it could be of importance if you might sell your custom menus. AutoCAD is now sold in many language formats. If your menu uses regular AutoCAD keywords such as LINE, CIRCLE, ARC, etc., preceding them with an underscore (_) will automatically translate these keywords into the language of the AutoCAD in use:

```
^c^c_line
```

Menu Magic

Have you ever noticed how the screen menu works from the user's point of view? At the top of every menu is the following:

```
AutoCAD
* * * *
```

At the bottom of most menus is the following:

```
SERVICE
LAST
```

Since these two sections appear on almost every user menu, it would be a waste of effort to write the code for every section. SERVICE and LAST are the last two items in the ***SCREEN section at the very bottom. As long as no other menu uses this area and does not have enough blank lines to interfere, SERVICE and LAST will appear on every menu. The only way to erase a previous menu is to have enough filled or blank lines to cover the previous menu.

When you look at the ** sections in the ACAD.MNU file you will notice a 3 following the section name. The 3 tells AutoCAD to begin this section on the third line down; in other words, the menu must leave the first two lines alone and unchanged. What's on these first two lines? Here's a copy of the beginning screen menu.

```
***SCREEN
**S
[AutoCAD ]^C^C^P(ai_rootmenus) ^P
[* * * * ]$S=ACAD.OSNAP
[FILE     ]$S=ACAD.01_FILE
[ASSIST   ]$S=ACAD.02_ASSIST
[VIEW     ]$S=ACAD.03_VIEW
[DRAW 1   ]$S=ACAD.04_DRAW1
[DRAW 2   ]$S=ACAD.05_DRAW2
[DRAW DIM]$S=ACAD.06_DRAWDIM
[CONSTRCT]$S=ACAD.07_CONSTRUCT
[MODIFY   ]$S=ACAD.08_MODIFY
[MOD DIM ]$S=ACAD.09_MODDIM
[DATA     ]$S=ACAD.10_DATA
[OPTIONS ]$S=ACAD.11_OPTIONS
[TOOLS    ]$S=ACAD.12_TOOLS

[HELP     ]$S=ACAD.13_HELP
```

(There are 8 blank lines between HELP and SERVICE.)

```
[SERVICE]$S=ACAD.service
[LAST    ]$S=ACAD.
```

When the ACAD.MNU file comes up the first time, the ***SCREEN is activated. The first two lines that appear on the screen menu are as follows:

```
AutoCAD
* * * *
```

As long as these two lines are never bothered, they'll always appear at the beginning of every user screen menu. This is why all user screen menus have a 3 following their names. It tells AutoCAD to begin the user menu on the third line so as not to disturb the first two lines.

Note: While doing the exercises in this book that relate to the screen menu, you must pick Preferences from the Options pull-down menu and then make sure the Screen Menu check box on the System page is checked (see Figure 3-1). Otherwise the screen menu will not be visible.

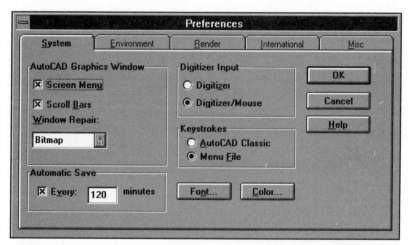

Figure 3-1: Screen Menu check box in the Preferences dialog box.

Menu Syntax

Look at the command that brings up the user screen menu:

```
[Special]^c^c$S=SPDRAW1
```

$S is the command that brings up a user screen menu. The $S call is to your user screen menu called SPDRAW1. **SPDRAW1 also begins on the third line to protect the first two lines. If you want to make sure that the previous menu is erased, make sure that your menu has about 18 to 20 lines, even if they are blank. The ***SCREEN menu SERVICE line begins on line 25. You should never have so many lines that it interferes with that one. Of course, yours should always begin the third line down.

The ability to overlay one menu with another gives you a lot of flexibility without increasing the size of the menu file. The ACAD.MNU is more than large enough as it is.

Another interesting feature is that any menu line item can access any other menu. Can you make the third button on your mouse bring down the **SPDRAW1 screen menu? Of course you can—if you change the second line on the ***AUX menu to the following:

```
***AUX1
;
^C^C$S=SPDRAW1
^C^C
^B
^O
^G
^D
^E
^T
```

Now when you press third button on the mouse, the **SPDRAW1 menu will appear.

Moving On

The AutoCAD menu structure may seem a little overwhelming at first, but once you get further into it, you'll see that it follows a logical progression. Take time to pause and regroup if you need to. The next chapter presents a tutorial that shows you how to create and change menus. As you work through the tutorial, the details will begin to come into focus.

4

How to
Make a Menu

CHAPTER 4

How to Make a Menu

The best way to understand how the AutoCAD menu structure works is to make a menu from scratch. The large AutoCAD menu structure is so big, it may seem intimidating and overwhelming at first. If you start with smaller menus, you can more easily see and understand the organization of the structure.

We are going to start with a simple screen menu. The screen menu was the basis and heart of the AutoCAD system from the beginning. With the current Windows/NT interface, most users will choose to turn the screen menu off. But learning how the screen menu works is the basis for all other menus. Therefore the first menu that we'll build will be a simple screen menu.

In order to work with the screen menu you must first make sure that it is turned on. To do this pick Preferences from the Options pull-down menu. Now make sure the Screen Menu check box is checked. (See Figure 4-1.)

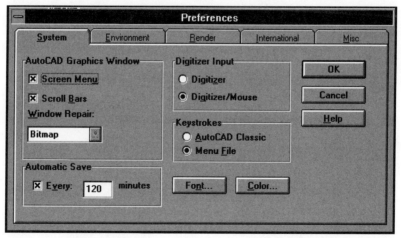

Figure 4-1: Screen Menu check box in the Preferences dialog box.

Building a New Menu

To begin a completely new menu, begin a new file using your choice of text editors as we have previously discussed. Call this file TEST.MNU. When you save this file, make sure you are saving it to the AutoCAD SUPPORT directory. In this way it will be easy for AutoCAD to call up with the

MENU command without having to search your directory file structure. This will probably be the C:\ACADR13\WIN\SUPPORT directory. Begin typing on the first line of the blank document the following two lines.

Type: ***SCREEN
      [ERASE L]^c^c(command "erase" "L" "")

    Whenever you see ^c^c in a menu it means to use the Shift+6 key, which produces the caret sign. Hold down the Shift key and press the number 6 on the typewriter keyboard, not the numeric keyboard. This is the menu symbol for Cancel.

    Now save your document. You should now have the TEST.MNU file saved in your SUPPORT directory. Return to AutoCAD.

    You've just created the simplest of menus. It has only two lines in it, but AutoCAD doesn't require that all menus be complex. Your new menu is called TEST. The line you placed in your menu after ***SCREEN will erase the last object you drew. (See Appendix B, "Using AutoLISP," for an explanation of how to express and construct simple AutoLISP commands that can be included in the menu structure.)

    You now need to load your menu.

Type: Menu <Enter>

    You will see the dialog box shown in Figure 4-2. (If you do not get a Select Menu File dialog box, make sure that the system variable FILEDIA is set to 1.)

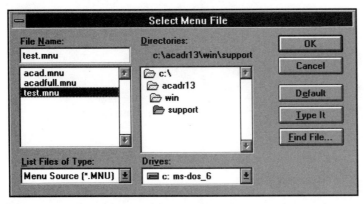

Figure 4-2: Select Menu File dialog box.

Pick TEST.MNU and OK. If you did not place your menu file in the SUPPORT directory, you will have to find the directory where your file is located. Your regular AutoCAD menu will now be replaced on the screen by your new menu. Notice that all of your pull-down menus are gone except for File and Help. All of your toolbars are also gone.

Draw a few lines on your screen. You'll have to enter **LINE**, since your regular menu is gone. Then pick the one and only menu item on your screen menu, Erase L. Immediately, the last object in your drawing is erased. Every time you pick the menu item, another object is erased.

Please note the following at this point: none of your buttons work except the Pick button; you have no pull-down menus; and your tablet doesn't work except in the screen area. The reason is that all these functions are controlled by the current menu in memory. The current menu is TEST.MNU, and there's nothing in it except the single line you just put there. As a result, none of the other menu functions are available to you.

If you save the existing drawing with the TEST.MNU as the saved base menu file, the next time you bring up the drawing with the TEST.MNU, the ACAD.MNL and ACADR13.LSP will not load and the many commands and much of AutoCAD will not be available. You can correct this problem by copying the ACAD.MNL file, generally found in the C:\ACADR13\COMMON\SUPPORT directory, to TEST.MNL. This way, TEST.MNL will load every time TEST.MNU loads.

Let's add to your menu. Return to your text editor and load TEST.MNU if it is not already loaded. Add the following lines to the beginning of your document.

Type:
```
***BUTTONS1
;

***BUTTONS2
^c^c(command "erase" "L" "")

***BUTTONS3
int,endp

***AUX1
;

***AUX2
^c^c(command "erase" "L" "")
```

```
***AUX3
int,endp

***SCREEN
[Erase L]^c^c(command "erase" "L" "")
```

This way, Button 2 will be Enter. Shift+Button 2 will be the ERASE LAST command and Ctrl+Button 2 will be the int,endp Object Snaps. You could go even further and use a ***BUTTONS4, and it would be Ctrl+Shift+Button 2. Now you can get a lot more options out of that single Button 2. Naturally, you can extend this technique by making these options available for other buttons.

Save your file. Now load the menu.

Type: Menu <Enter>

Pick TEST.MNU and OK. The menu looks the same as before. But the difference is that you've added a definition to your buttons. The first button is still Pick. The second button is the same as Enter, indicated by the ; (semicolon) on the first line after ***BUTTONS1 or ***AUX1. (The semicolon is AutoCAD's macro language for Enter.) The Shift of the second button is Erase Last and the Ctrl of the second button is your Object Snap intersection or endpoint. Since the Shift of the second button is exactly the same as the line that appears in the ***SCREEN section you can either pick from the screen menu to erase the last entity or use the Shift of the second button on your mouse.

Try it out. Draw a few lines on your screen. Remember, you'll have to enter **LINE**. Then press the Shift second button. Each time you press the button, an object will be erased, exactly as it was when you picked the screen menu command.

Test out the Ctrl of the second button. Hold the Ctrl key down while in a LINE command and immediately the Object Snap intersection or end point will be active.

The familiar Object Snap rectangle should now appear on your cross-hairs. As you can see, this is an extremely productive use of buttons on your mouse. Object Snap is one of the most important tools for accuracy in AutoCAD. It's also the least efficiently selected command in AutoCAD. If each Object Snap selection were attached to a mouse button or combination of Shift, Ctrl or Shift+Ctrl, you could easily select from them at will while in any of AutoCAD's commands.

With Release 13 you have another option, which comes as the default. This is the cursor menu, which is defined as your Object Snap picks. Out of the box, it is defined as Button 3 or Shift+Button 2. Later we'll show you how to create and manipulate more cursor menus.

Let's now construct a complete menu. Return to your text editor and the TEST.MNU file. Your file as listed should currently look like this:

```
***BUTTONS1
;
***BUTTONS2
^c^c(command "erase" "L" "")

***BUTTONS3
int,endp

***AUX1
;

***AUX2
^c^c(command "erase" "L" "")

***AUX3
int,endp

***SCREEN
[Erase L]^c^c(command "erase" "L" "")
```

Erase the last line from the menu. And then continue the following under ***SCREEN.

```
[AutoCAD ]
[* * * * ]
[FILE    ]
[ASSIST  ]
[VIEW    ]
[DRAW 1  ]
[DRAW 2  ]
[DRAW DIM]
[CONSTRCT]
```

```
[MODIFY  ]
[MOD DIM ]
[DATA    ]
[OPTIONS ]
[TOOLS   ]
[MYMENU]$S=SPDRAW

[HELP    ]
```

(Do not type what is in these parentheses. Insert seven blank lines between HELP and SERVICE.)

```
[SERVICE]
[LAST   ]$S=
**SPDRAW 3
[LINE]^C^CLine
[PLINE]^C^CPline
[CIRCLE]^C^CCircle
[ARC]^C^CArc
[MTEXT]^C^CMtext
[ZOOM W]'Zoom W
[ZOOM P]'Zoom P
[ZOOM A]'^C^CView R ZA
[ERASE W]^C^CErase W
[ERASE L]^C^C(command "erase" "L" "")
[COPY]^C^CCopy
[MOVE]^C^CMove
[OFFSET]^C^COffset
[PEDIT]^C^CPedit
[BREAK F]^C^C(command "break" pause "f")
[INSERT]^C^CDdinsert
[LAYER]^C^CDdlmodes
[SAVE]^C^CQsave
```

Let's analyze the sections. ***BUTTONS and ***AUX of course define your buttons and their meanings. ***SCREEN begins the screen section.

```
[AutoCAD]^C^C$S=SCREEN
```

This is the first line of every AutoCAD submenu. It brings you back to the root screen menu. If the menu structure is done correctly, these first two lines will never accidentally be erased.

```
[* * * *]
```

This line brings up an Object Snap submenu in the real ACAD.MNU. In our TEST menu nothing will happen, since we haven't written the submenus. These lines are in the ACAD.MNU file. They're shown here only to demonstrate a more complete menu system without having to type in the entire file or what each item does.

The rest of the ***SCREEN section is there only to show the brackets.

```
[MYMENU]$S=SPDRAW
```

This last line in the section calls the **SPDRAW menu that we've written. This exercise is only a sample of what can be done; but its usefulness can be incorporated in the ACAD.MNU file.

```
[LAST    ]$S=
```

Notice how the [LAST] menu item works. $S= is not followed by anything. This causes the menu to go back to the last menu it was working on. Each time this is picked it goes back to one previous menu until it has no more to go back to, then nothing happens.

Organizing Your Menus

Do you use certain AutoCAD commands more than others? Do you use others only two or three times per drawing session? Do you use some commands all the time? Competitive CAD systems that organize their menus according to useful function claim advantage over AutoCAD's alphabetical menu structure. However, this advantage has limited value, since AutoCAD's menu structures can be changed, whereas competitive systems' structures cannot.

The best approach in organizing your menus is to use the time-honored 20/80 rule: You use only 20 percent of anything 80 percent of the time. With that principle in mind, why not put the most frequently used AutoCAD commands on one menu, regardless of whether they are draw, edit or display commands?

This is what the **SPDRAW menu does:

```
**SPDRAW 3
[LINE]^C^CLine
[PLINE]^C^CPline
[CIRCLE]^C^CCircle
[ARC]^C^CArc
[MTEXT]^C^CMtext
[ZOOM W]'Zoom W
[ZOOM P]'Zoom P
[ZOOM A]'^C^CView R ZA
[ERASE W]^C^CErase W
[ERASE L]^C^C(command "erase" "L" "")
[COPY]^C^CCopy
[MOVE]^C^CMove
[OFFSET]^C^COffset
[PEDIT]^C^CPedit
[BREAK F]^C^C(command "break" pause "f")
[INSERT]^C^CDdinsert
[LAYER]^C^CDdlmodes
[SAVE]^C^CQsave
```

This is the submenu section we wrote. It has 18 of the most commonly used AutoCAD commands. It begins **SPDRAW 3. The 3 instructs our menu to begin on the third line down; this reserves space for the first two permanent lines. We can use simple AutoCAD commands or complex AutoLISP programs. This is not meant to necessarily include your most frequently used commands. This should be your decision. This is only an example of how the most useful AutoCAD commands can be incorporated on a single menu area to add productivity.

Try out your new menu. Save it as TEST.MNU as before, then load the menu in AutoCAD.

Type: Menu <Enter>

Pick TEST.MNU in the Select Menu File dialog box and pick OK.

Now it's starting to look like a real menu. In fact, it's beginning to look like the ACAD.MNU. Of course, it's not totally functional; it's used simply as an exercise. Try picking any of the regular AutoCAD items and notice that nothing happens. Pick the MYMENU item. It should immediately take you to the SPDRAW menu that contains the various AutoCAD commands. Try out a few, and see if they work. LAST will work but SERVICE will not. If you pick AutoCAD, it should return you to the main root screen menu.

If your screen menu is not operating properly or you're getting some strange things on the screen, go back and check the file to see if it's written correctly. Working with menus can be very tricky, and even minor mistakes can keep the menus from working. It is also possible that it didn't compile correctly. If this is the case delete TEST.MNS, TEST.MNC and TEST.MNR. This will force a complete recompilation of the entire menu.

Through this exercise you've learned a lot about how a menu is put together from scratch. But it's not our intention to write additional menus. One of the current advantages of AutoCAD is that the entire menu system can be incorporated in one single file or a series of loadable pull-down menus added to a single base menu. AutoCAD doesn't set a physical limit on the size of your menu file or any of the loadable files.

So what would you do to put our special drawing menu **SPDRAW in the real AutoCAD file? Let's try it and see. Before you begin, be sure you have a good backup copy of your ACAD.MNU file. An easy way to do this is to copy it to another file name in the same directory. As a general rule, don't ever work on a menu that's important to you without first making a copy of its most recent version.

Now edit your ACAD.MNU file. If it will not fit in Notepad for Windows you might try Write for Windows. Be sure not to convert the file and to save it as a text file. In addition, you must leave the file by starting a new file so that Write does not still control the file when AutoCAD wants to open it.

Search for ***SCREEN in your file. The following is the AutoCAD ***SCREEN section.

```
***SCREEN
**S
[AutoCAD ]^C^C^P(ai_rootmenus) ^P
[* * * * ]$S=ACAD.OSNAP
[FILE    ]$S=ACAD.01_FILE
[ASSIST  ]$S=ACAD.02_ASSIST
[VIEW    ]$S=ACAD.03_VIEW
[DRAW 1  ]$S=ACAD.04_DRAW1
[DRAW 2  ]$S=ACAD.05_DRAW2
[DRAW DIM]$S=ACAD.06_DRAWDIM
[CONSTRCT]$S=ACAD.07_CONSTRUCT
[MODIFY  ]$S=ACAD.08_MODIFY
[MOD DIM ]$S=ACAD.09_MODDIM
[DATA    ]$S=ACAD.10_DATA
[OPTIONS ]$S=ACAD.11_OPTIONS
[TOOLS   ]$S=ACAD.12_TOOLS
```

Add the following line immediately after [TOOLS].

Type: `[*DRAW*] $S=SPDRAW`

[*DRAW*] and SPDRAW are names you make up. [*DRAW*] is how the name will appear on your screen menu. SPDRAW is your subsection name.

You now must find a place to put the **SPDRAW section. It can be placed anywhere within the menu. A good place to put it is immediately before some other ** section. Placing it before another ** section assures that you're not stepping on some other section within the menu. Therefore page down in your text editor until you find the first ** section and insert the **SPDRAW section there.

If you have not saved the previous **SPDRAW section, type in the following lines (they're the same as those in the **SPDRAW section on your TEST.MNU file):

Type: ```
**SPDRAW 3
[LINE]^C^CLine
[PLINE]^C^CPline
[CIRCLE]^C^CCircle
[ARC]^C^CArc
[MTEXT]^C^CMtext
[ZOOM W]'Zoom W
[ZOOM P]'Zoom P
[ZOOM A]'^C^CView R ZA
[ERASE W]^C^CErase W
[ERASE L]^C^C(command "erase" "L" "")
[COPY]^C^CCopy
[MOVE]^C^CMove
[OFFSET]^C^COffset
[PEDIT]^C^CPedit
[BREAK F]^C^C(command "break" pause "f")
[INSERT]^C^CDdinsert
[LAYER]^C^CDdlmodes
[SAVE]^C^CQsave
```

Save the ACAD.MNU file and exit from the text editor. Load the new menu.

Type:  `Menu <Enter>`

From the Select Menu File dialog box pick ACAD.MNU and OK. Now you're using the real AutoCAD menu file. Everything should work as before, but there's one addition. On the root screen menu is the DRAW option. Pick this option, and you should have access to your new special menu. Pick either AutoCAD or LAST, and it will return you to the root screen menu.

Check out your menu carefully. Make sure everything is working properly. If the main menu screen looks funny, that's your first "trouble" clue. If anything is wrong with your menu, restore the backup to the ACAD.MNU file that you created and begin again. It's easier to begin from a place you know is right than to try to fix something that's hopelessly wrong. *Be very careful when working with the AutoCAD menu.* It's so large and complex that shifting even one line out of sequence can cause the entire menu, or major sections of it, not to work.
```

Moving On

 Congratulations. You've now learned the basics of menu construction, and you have successfully altered and added to your menu file. But this is only the beginning. There are many other things you can do to make AutoCAD more productive. In Chapter 5, we'll show you how you can make your digitizer even more efficient by customizing the tablet menus.

5

Making
Tablet
Menus

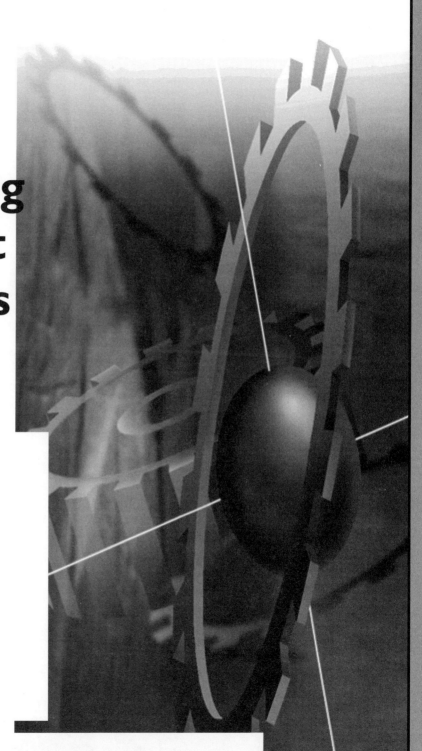

Making Tablet Menus

Screen menus are all well and good, but they're not the most productive way to enter AutoCAD commands. A single pick on a tablet menu can take the place of several picks from the screen menu. Although tablet menus are very productive, the growth of the graphical user interface in AutoCAD and the popularity of Release 13 and the Windows/NT environment have made tablet menus less important than they once were. More AutoCAD users are opting to use the standard mouse. The customizable toolbars have contributed to the current decline in popularity that digitizers and tablet menus once enjoyed. But if you *have* chosen to use the tablet menu with AutoCAD, you should learn how to make it as efficient as possible.

Modifying the Tablet Menu

While maintaining the basic commands on the tablet menu, you can feel free to modify their underlying meanings. For instance, it may be more efficient to change all Object Snap commands to Object Snap Mode commands, using (setvar). Another example: (setvar "osmode" 1) will permanently set the Object Snap to endpoint until the next Object Snap is chosen. Or a third suggestion: a general ERASE command can be made more specific. These are simple alterations that you can make without customizing the menu beyond the recognition of others who may use your system.

The AutoCAD tablet is divided into four menu areas (see Figure 5-1). The real customization is done in tablet menu Area 1. Areas 2, 3 and 4 are reserved for the standard tablet. Area 1, at the top of the tablet menu, is capable of holding 200 to 300 blocks. This is where your special macros and parts should be placed.

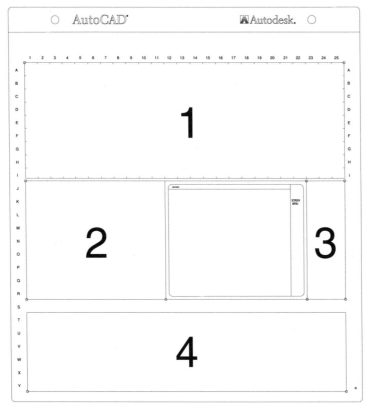

Figure 5-1: Basic tablet menu.

Tablet Area I

The standard AutoCAD tablet menu is divided into four menu areas, as illustrated in Figure 5-1. We're going to concentrate on the first area.

Notice on the tablet that the area is labeled A through I down the side and 1 through 25 across the top. This creates a crossgrid of 225 blocks on the menu. By using this crossgrid method, you can name each block—for example, A-1, B-1, G-17, etc. In the ACAD.MNU file, there's an area with corresponding labels.

The four areas that hold the tablet area for the menu file are ***TABLET sections. Generally, they're called ***TABLET1, ***TABLET2, ***TABLET3 and ***TABLET4. But these actual names are not required. More on that later. For now, let's look at the ACAD.MNU. Load the ACAD.MNU file in your text editor. Now search for ***TABLET1. You should see something like the following.

```
***TABLET1
**TABLET1STD
[A-1]
[A-2]
[A-3]
[A-4]
[A-5]
[A-6]
[A-7]
[A-8]
[A-9]
```

If you want to place a command in Block A-1, you should modify the line containing [A-1]. What should you put here? You have a number of options. It could be other AutoCAD commands, similar to what you did on the screen menu. But more than likely you'll want to enter your own AutoLISP programs or blocks you'll be inserting.

Make a BLOCK or WBLOCK and call it PART1. Here's how you create an automatic insert routine that places PART1 in your drawing without your having to do anything but pick the A-1 portion of the menu. To the right of [A-1] begin the following:

Type: `^C^C(command "insert" "part1" pause "1" "1" "0") <Enter>`

This AutoLISP statement will insert part1, then pause to let you pick a point. The "1," "1" and "0" are the scale factors and the rotation. The end result is that you pick A-1 on the tablet, and the block appears. Then pick where you want the block to be inserted.

Save the file and exit the text editor. Now load the ACAD menu.

Type: `Menu <Enter>`

Pick ACAD.MNU and OK. To test your new menu entry, all you have to do is pick the A-1 of the tablet.

Let's emphasize a few things here. First, there is nothing magical about [A-1] or any of the headers for the tablet area. In fact, they don't even have to be there. But it's best not to erase them, as you'll see in a moment. Because they're in brackets, they don't do anything except point to where the appropriate line is at any time. (Remember that menu items in brackets are not executable.) Since this is not a screen menu, nothing is going to appear on the screen or anywhere else. But if you leave the headers, it gives you the opportunity to flag which line is which.

If you ever erase one of the bracketed items or add a line in this area, you'll throw off the items by the number of lines added or deleted.

Creating Tablet Underlays

Now that you know how to set up the menu systems for tablets, how do you create the underlay and symbols to put under the template so that it will properly line up when you pick? This is the easy part. Using Auto-CAD, create a crossgrid similar to Figure 5-2. Make each block exactly .4 inch in each direction. Save the drawing as your model. Now ZOOM in on each of the blocks and draw whatever you want in the appropriate block. (Of course, save the updated model each time you change it.) Plot the crossgrid with your symbols at 1=1. Cut it down and place it either on top of the tablet or under the transparent area.

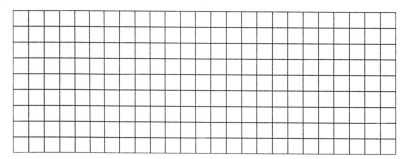

Figure 5-2: Tablet Area 1 crossgrid.

Super-Large Digitizer Tablets

The standard AutoCAD tablet menu is designed for an approximately 11- x 11-inch tablet. What if you have an 11- x 17-inch tablet? Could you use the extra area for tablet menus? Yes, indeed.

The size of the tablet menu areas and the number of squares in each area depend upon the TABLET command in AutoCAD. When you enter the TABLET command, choose the CFG suboption. You're asked to pick the upper left, lower left and lower right points that outline the tablet area. (See Figure 5-3.) Then you tell AutoCAD how many columns and rows you want the area divided into.

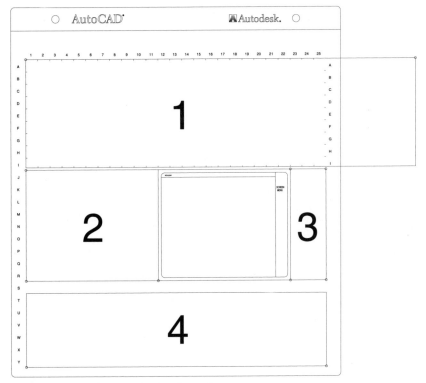

Figure 5-3: Expanded Tablet Area 1.

When working with a larger tablet, move the lower right point to the far right point of the larger tablet. When asked the number of columns, increase the number from 25 to however many you want. Obviously, if you decrease the number of columns in a larger area, the individual squares are larger. Therefore, you have to develop your own mathematics as to the physical dimensions of the tablet area and how many squares you're allocating.

Moving On

As you know, our goal is productivity. You've learned from this chapter that this often translates to reducing several commands and picks into a single pick, making the process of CAD so transparent that you can concentrate on design and drafting.

Now let's move on and look at more ways to create and use menus by looking at the graphical user interface and its ability to let you provide visual onscreen menus—especially those pull-downs. Later in the book we'll go a step further, with cascading and cursor menus as well as tool-bars. But first let's cover the basics.

6

The Advanced
User Interface

The Advanced User Interface

Beginning with Release 9, AutoCAD introduced a new menu concept called Advanced User Interface. This has evolved into a totally Windows-compliant graphical user interface with pull-down menus and customizable toolbars.

Over the years, AutoCAD's user interface has received some bad press. It developed a reputation for being hard to learn and hard to use. Of course, most of this criticism was generated by its competitors or by others who weren't using AutoCAD. But because perception often supersedes reality, Autodesk has put a lot of effort over the last several years into creating an easy-to-use, consistent interface. In Release 13 they have really outdone themselves.

Since AutoCAD is a graphics package, it seems only natural that it should include a graphical user interface. Since AutoCAD is now totally incorporated within the Windows/NT environment, where all programs operate in a similar manner, it's easy to switch among them and still feel at home.

But just because an interface feature is available, it may not necessarily be the most productive method for accomplishing a given task. For example, the pull-down menu feature doesn't guarantee more productivity when it's used as it comes from the box.

The Advanced User Interface includes five elements:

- Menu bar
- Pull-down menus
- Image tile menus
- Dialog boxes
- Toolbars

Let's look first at these five areas and analyze the pros and cons of each.

Menu Bar

The menu bar is located at the top of the screen. (See Figure 6-1.) The benefit of using a menu bar is that it takes up a lot less room than the traditional right-side screen menu. Theoretically, you should be able to completely replace the right-side screen menu with the top menu bar.

You can't do this when you're using AutoCAD right out of the box; you'd first need to make some alterations. But with Release 13's cascading menus, this is becoming more of a possibility.

					AutoCAD -	
<u>F</u>ile	<u>E</u>dit	<u>V</u>iew	<u>D</u>ata	<u>O</u>ptions	<u>T</u>ools	<u>H</u>elp

Figure 6-1: Menu bar.

If you choose to use the standard ACAD.MNU file, you will find hardly any AutoCAD commands on the menu bar's pull-down menus. Therefore the basic menu bar doesn't substitute for the screen menu or tablet menu. As you will see, the toolbars more than make up for this.

If you want the more traditional Release 12 menu bar back, you can always load ACADFULL.MNU. I think you will find that the new interface means you won't need to do that, especially if you create at least one pull-down for your 20/80 rule commands—the 20 percent of commands that you use 80 percent of the time.

If you want to, then, how do you turn off the right-side screen menu? This part is easy. Choose Preferences from the Options pull-down menu, and then make certain that the Screen Menu check box in the Preferences dialog box is *not* checked.

Pull-Down Menus

When you pick one of the menu bar items, a screen usually appears superimposed on your drawing. (See Figure 6-2.) This gives the illusion of pulling down a menu just as you'd pull down a window shade. The pull-down screen lists a series of commands for you to choose from. After you've picked a command, the pull-down menu "rolls back up" and disappears.

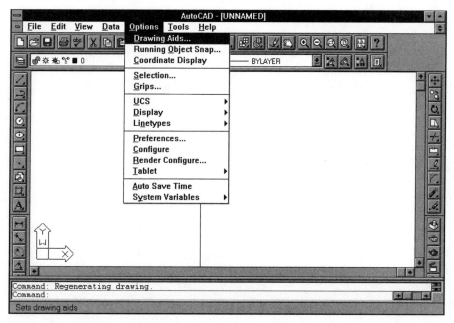

Figure 6-2: Pull-down menu.

Viewing commands on pull-down menus is much faster than paging through 20 screen menu commands at a time. Each pull-down menu can be made almost the size of the entire screen. This gives you the ability to fully describe the menu option. Each command can include more than 70 characters, if necessary. (Even though this is possible, it's usually not desirable; the last thing you need is all that reading each time you select a menu item.)

Because the menus are pulled down over your drawing, you can keep your eyes on the screen, which makes for better concentration. The only major drawback to pull-down menus is that they're not complete.

As pull-down menus become more common, they're falling into the same trap as the right-side screen menus; in order to get everything onto the menus, programmers are including more menu options rather than the single pick necessary to issue the command or perform the function. This is why toolbars are so much more convenient—they give you the single pick for each of the major options.

In addition, without a screen menu, the user does not have access to options that can generally be picked from the screen menu. Pull-down menus do not allow for additional options to be picked, since the pull-down menu is no longer on the screen once the initial pick is made. Many commercial programs, and other Autodesk programs, solve this problem through dialog boxes.

Image Tile Menus

The introduction of images to replace menu text is an important innovation for boosting efficiency. (See Figure 6-3.) Image tile menus have great potential, but unfortunately too few users take the time to understand them and customize them for increased productivity.

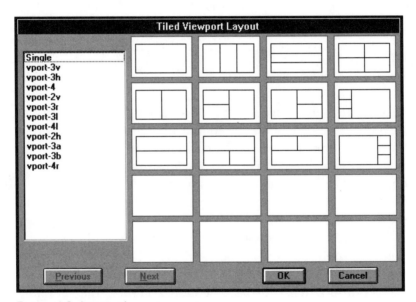

Figure 6-3: Image tile menu.

Image tile menus contain graphics-type pictures (image tiles) that represent menu items. When you choose an image from your screen, you're picking a menu item. This menu item may be a simple AutoCAD command, an entire AutoLISP program or anything in between. The advantage of images is that the mind's eye can interpret a picture more quickly and better than it can process a string of words.

Unfortunately, there aren't many built-in image tiles available with AutoCAD. Many AutoCAD users think the image tiles that come with

AutoCAD are the only ones available, and now that AutoCAD uses toolbars and dialog boxes, it doesn't rely on image tile menus as much. The advantage of image tiles is that you can pick a picture that resembles a block instead of having to remember the name of the block. Although you can do this with toolbars, it's easier to have a picture of the block in an image tile menu than it is to create a unique toolbar icon.

The only negative factor about using image tiles is that you can't control their size, number and placement when you're compiling. In Release 13, you're limited to the option of providing up to 20 images per screen. Yet, if the image tile menus were like menu squares on a tablet, you would be able to control the size, number and placement variables.

Dialog Boxes

Dialog boxes are among the most valuable productivity tools available in AutoCAD; they let you interact with the program, hence their name. A dialog box can give you a simple message, such as telling you that a file is not found. It can ask you to "Pick OK or Return to acknowledge." It can also show you every layer and its status in your drawing. Other dialog boxes help you move around your hard disk.

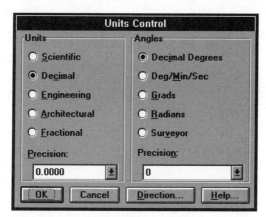

Figure 6-4: Example of a dialog box.

A file dialog box will appear any time you issue an AutoCAD command that requires you to enter the name of a file, such as the following:

- SAVE
- VSLIDE, MSLIDE
- DXBIN, DXFIN, IGESIN, DXFOUT
- ATTEXT
- LOAD
- MENU
- SCRIPT
- STYLE
- WBLOCK

Some commands—for instance, INSERT—can access a file dialog box if you ask for one with a ~ (tilde), even if you're not using the DDINSERT command. You can also prevent a dialog box from appearing: If you set the system variable FILEDIA to 0, no file dialog box will appear and the questions will be asked at the command line.

Another type of dialog box alerts you to an invalid entry, such as "file not found."

There are several drawbacks with dialog boxes. Some, such as those that set Snap and Grid, are too time-consuming; much of the status information they offer can be determined straight from the status line, and the modes can be set much faster by typing. And when you need to toggle, function keys and control keys are superior to dialog boxes.

Dialog boxes are totally customizable. Good third-party software now depends heavily on dialog boxes because of their superior user interface.

Toolbars

The advent of customizable toolbars is probably the most productive addition to the AutoCAD interface to come along in years. This is the first time Autodesk has created a truly user-modifiable menu system from within AutoCAD. As you've seen, all of the other menus are changed through text editors outside of AutoCAD. This is going to change the look and feel of each and every AutoCAD station as users reposition the toolbars and change them for their own productivity.

Figure 6-5: Example of a toolbar.

Customizing Your Menus

The rest of this chapter concentrates on how to develop and customize your menu bar and pull-down menus. The exercises in this chapter relate to the general concept of the pull-down menu and rely on modifying the base ACAD.MNU file. Once you thoroughly understand this, you will understand the material in Chapter 10 on the loadable pull-down menu— a pull-down menu that can be created and left in its own file. The loadable pull-down menu is loaded onto whatever base menu you choose without having to modify the base menu.

The easiest way to see how the pull-down menus are organized is to look at the AutoCAD menu itself. Use your text editor and bring up the ACAD.MNU file. Search for ***POP5 in your file. The following is a portion of the ***POP5 menu.

```
***POP5
ID_Options [&Options]
ID_Dwgaids [&Drawing Aids…]'_ddrmodes
ID_Osndd   [Running &Object Snap…]'_ddosnap
ID_Cordis  [&Coordinate Display]^D
           [--]
ID_Ddselec [&Selection…]'_ddselect
ID_Ddgrips [&Grips…]'_ddgrips
```

Every pull-down menu uses ***POP plus its designated number. Above is an example of a portion of Pull-down Menu 5. Pull-down Menu 7 would be ***POP7. Like tablet and screen menus, the major section numbers are preceded by ***. They're similar to screen menus in that the words surrounded by brackets appear as titles in the pull-down. But unlike screen menus, they're not as limited in the number of characters allowed. The width of a pull-down menu depends on the space required by the largest item in brackets. Of course, it can't extend beyond the screen itself.

The first line below the ***POP5 is the title that appears in the menu bar when you first move the cursor into the top of the screen. In this case, the title is Options. When you pick Options, the menu drops down and you see what is in brackets. The & is placed before the letter that is the shortcut key for that item. The item beginning with ID_ is the symbol label for the menu item. To the right of the menu item is the command that will be executed.

Let's write our own pull-down menu similar to the SPDRAW screen menu from Chapter 4. Search for ***POP7. Once you find it, move to the bottom of the menu before the introduction of the Toolbars section. This is where you will insert your pull-down menu, which will be called ***POP8. After the seventh menu enter the following.

Type:
```
***POP8
[&Special]
[&Line]^C^Cline
[&Pline]^C^Cpline
[&Circle]^C^Ccircle
[&Arc]^C^Carc
[M&text]^C^Cmtext
[Zoom &W]'zoom W
[Zo&om P]'zoom P
[&Zoom A]'^C^Czoom A
[&Erase W]^C^Cerase W
[Erase &L]^C^C(command "erase" "L" "")
[Cop&y]^C^Ccopy
[Mo&ve]^C^Cmove
[O&ffset]^C^Coffset
[Pe&dit]^C^Cpedit
```

```
[&Break F]^C^C(command "break" pause "f")
[&Insert...]^C^Cddinsert
[Laye&r...]^C^Cddlmodes
[&Save]^C^Cqsave
```

Make certain you add one blank line at the end. This is used by Auto-CAD to determine the end of the pull-down menu. Save your menu and exit the text editor.

You now need to load your menu.

Type: `Menu <Enter>`

Pick ACAD.MNU and OK. Your new menu is now loaded. Try it out by picking Special from the menu bar. This is the new pull-down you just created.

Moving On

With Release 13, AutoCAD has made great improvements on its overall menu system. But that doesn't mean you have to stop there. You need to learn how to use the pull-down menus to serve your own discipline in the most efficient way possible. Don't just accept what's there. This is an area where good planning can really pay off. In the next chapter you'll learn more about AutoCAD's menu system, with a discussion of pull-down menus that includes cascading and cursor menus.

7

Cascading Menus & Cursor Menus

Cascading Menus & Cursor Menus

Productive menus that make your work easier are important, and AutoCAD has made many productivity enhancements over the years. As you work through this chapter, you'll learn new techniques for creating exciting visual menu options, as opposed to the simple pull-down menus in other AutoCAD releases. Welcome to cascading and cursor menus—activated through the graphical user interface (GUI).

Cascading menus, although attached to the menu bar, work like the old pull-down menus but flow over each other to provide fuller on-screen options. They decrease the number of picks necessary to start your command but also show you all the options on the screen, no matter how deeply they're nested. Unlike the old menus, there are no Previous and Next picks.

Cursor menus, on the other hand, are not attached to the menu bar and are a different type of pull-down menu. The cursor menu is activated by a mouse button of your choice and appears onscreen wherever the mouse crosshairs intersect. This gives you a heads-up menu system—you don't even have to move the cursor off your drawing to pick a command. It's one of the fastest pull-down menus available, and it's right where it should be—at your fingertips with your cursor.

You'll find programming for both of these menus reasonably simple, once you've learned a few basic rules. Your confidence will grow, as will your visual custom menu options. This chapter shows you how these menus work, how to build your own, even how to have as many cursor menus as you want. You'll have lightning-fast access to your AutoCAD and AutoLISP commands.

Cascading Menus

Beginning with AutoCAD Release 12, many improvements in pull-down menus were made, one of which is the *cascading menu.* You'll see a cascading menu immediately when you select a pull-down menu with a choice that has a right arrowhead symbol after it. This symbol means that this choice contains more options. After you pick a cascading menu, if any other options exist, they, too, will have an arrowhead beside them.

As you can imagine, this is a much better option than simply nesting pull-down menus. For one thing, it's faster; and, because it's visual, you always know where you are in the nest and can see the level above you.

Cascading menus are easy to create if you know how to create a simple pull-down menu. Let's look at the components of a cascading menu. (The line numbers 1–20 are provided as references only so that we can describe the function of each line below; the line numbers are *not* part of the actual menu system.)

```
 1    ***POP1
 2    [XXXXX]
 3    [->XXXXX]
 4        [XXXXX]
 5        [XXXXX]
 6        [<-XXXXX]
 7    [--]
 8    [->XXXXX]
 9        [->XXXXX]
10            [XXXXX]
11            [XXXXX]
12            [<-XXXXX]
13        [XXXXX]
14        [<-XXXXX]
15    [--]
16    [->XXXXX]
17        [->XXXXX]
18            [XXXXX]
19            [XXXXX]
20            [<-<-XXXXX]
```

Below are descriptions of each of the lines of code above, referenced by the number to the left of each line of code.

1	This begins the pull-down menu as item POP1. It begins with three asterisks (***), as it is a major section.
2	This is the name of the pull-down menu. The name on the menu bar appears in brackets. No command may be attached to this line.
3	This line begins a single-level cascading menu. Notice that it begins with a hyphen and a greater-than symbol (->). No command should be attached to this label—it references itself to lines 4, 5 and 6.
4–6	These are the actual cascading menu lines. The commands will be appended to these lines after the brackets. In addition to being a cascading menu line, line 6 has a special purpose: the less-than symbol and the hyphen (<-) preceding the label indicate that it's the last line of the cascading menu.
7	Two hyphens in brackets by themselves draw a separator line in the pull-down menu. You may not use any other character in the brackets. Separator lines, of course, are optional.
8, 9	Line 8 begins a cascading menu, just as line 3 does. The difference here is that line 9 also introduces its own cascading menu under line 8. Notice that each line begins with a hyphen and a greater-than symbol (->). No command should be attached to these labels.
9, 13, 14	These are the lines under the first-level cascading menu begun on line 8.
10–12	These lines belong to the second-level cascading menu begun on line 9. In addition to being a second-level cascading-menu line, line 12 also closes the second-level cascading menu. Note the less-than symbol and hyphen (<-) preceding the label.

14   Line 14 closes the first-level cascading menu begun on line 8 (note the <- preceding the label).

15   Two hyphens in brackets by themselves draw a separator line in the pull-down menu. You may not use any other character in the brackets. Separator lines, of course, are optional.

16–20   These lines are almost identical to lines 8 through 14 (they open and close two cascading menus), with one exception: line 20 closes both the second-level and the first-level cascading menus, since there are no additional lines. Notice the two "closing" symbols (<-<-) on line 20. (Remember that you can have many levels of cascading menus open. You need to use a <- for each level you need to close.)

Now let's look at an example of a cascading menu you might create, called TEST2.MNU. So we can see exactly what's going on in this menu, we'll include only its pull-down (POP) lines.

Type in the following to the new TEST2.MNU file that you create using your text editor:

```
***POP16
[Dialog Boxes]
[->Editing Boxes]
  [->Change]
    [Group Properties...]^c^cddchprop
    [<-Single Object...]^c^cddmodify
  [Edit Line Text...]^c^cddedit
  [<-Rename...]^c^cddrename
[--]
[->Settings]
  [Object Creation...]^c^cddemodes
  [Selection Settings...]^c^cddselect
  [Grips...]^c^cddgrips
  [Layers...]^c^cddlmodes
  [Object Snaps...]^c^cddosnap
  [Points Style...]^c^cddptype
  [Units...]^c^cddunits
  [<-Drawing Aids...]^c^cddrmodes
[--]
```

```
[->Display]
  [Views...]^c^cddview
  [->UCS...]
    [UCS Basic...]^c^cdducs
    [<-UCS Right Angle]^c^cdducsp
  [<-Viewpoints...]^c^cddvpoint
[--]
[->Attributes]
  [Define...]^c^cddattdef
  [Edit...]^c^cddatte
  [<-Extract...]^c^cddattext
[--]
[Filters...]'filter
[Insert...]^c^cddinsert
[Plot...]^c^cplot
```

This is a convenient pull-down menu that we will expand later in this chapter. In one central location, it lists most of the dialog boxes available with Release 13.

Once you've created the above TEST2.MNU and saved it as a text file, load the menu.

Type: MENU \<Enter>

A file dialog box should appear. Find the directory where TEST2.MNU is stored. Now pick TEST2 and OK.

All other menus should be blank and there should be only one pull-down menu available. Notice that it is on the far left-hand side. You called it ***POP16. It isn't positioned as the sixteenth menu toward the right because there's only one menu. The numbers given to the pull-down menus are sequentially positioned. For example, if you had three menus numbered 4, 9 and 11, they would be in that order from left to right. The numbers are arbitrary but are sequential in relation to each other. You may even skip numbers. The menus you create will appear in numerical order, but no space will be left for missing numbers. Figure 7-1 is an example of what your pull-down menu will look like with the Editing Boxes cascading.

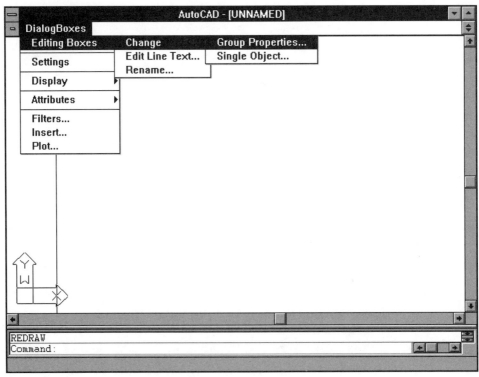

Figure 7-1: Sample cascading menu.

Cursor Menus

Cursor menus are a special type of pull-down menu that you can access onscreen at your cursor position instead of pulling down from the menu bar. Since cursor menus are assigned to a pick button instead of the pull-down menu bar, they're quickly and easily accessible—and your cursor is right where it needs to be.

Since a cursor menu is just a special type of pull-down menu, it follows the same rules; for instance, it's created and titled as pull-down menus are, and it can have cascading menus. Following, however, are some specific rules for cursor menus:

- The cursor menu is named ***POP0. (It must be preceded by three asterisks.)
- You must have at least one regular pull-down menu in your .MNU file, such as ***POP1. Its number and content don't matter.
- The cursor menu should be assigned to a button so it will pop up at the cursor.

Let's modify TEST2.MNU to demonstrate how easy it is to make a pull-down menu into a cursor menu. You'll add the ***BUTTONS1 and ***AUX1 sections and the ***POP1 section. Notice that the cursor menu is assigned to pick Button 2 with $p0=* (the command that makes a pull-down menu appear is the first line after ***BUTTONS1 and ***AUX1—thus it's assigned to Button 2). Remember that the reason for both ***BUTTONS1 and ***AUX1 is to keep them in sync for both the digitizer puck and the mouse buttons. Notice that all you are doing to the file is adding the ***BUTTONS, ***AUX and ***POP1 items, then changing the name of ***POP16 to ***POP0. Here is the complete TEST2.MNU listing.

```
***BUTTONS1
$p0=*

***POP1
[DRAW]
[Line]^c^cline

***POP0
[Dialog Boxes]
[->Editing Boxes]
  [->Change]
    [Group Properties...]^c^cddchprop
    [<-Single Object...]^c^cddmodify
  [Edit Line Text...]^c^cddedit
  [<-Rename...]^c^cddrename
```

```
[--]
[->Settings]
  [Object Creation...]^c^cddemodes
  [Selection Settings...]^c^cddselect
  [Grips...]^c^cddgrips
  [Layers...]^c^cddlmodes
  [Object Snaps...]^c^cddosnap
  [Points Style...]^c^cddptype
  [Units...]^c^cddunits
  [<-Drawing Aids...]^c^cddrmodes
[--]
[->Display]
  [Views...]^c^cddview
  [->UCS...]
    [UCS Basic...]^c^cdducs
    [<-UCS Right Angle]^c^cdducsp
  [<-Viewpoints...]^c^cddvpoint
[--]
[->Attributes]
  [Define...]^c^cddattdef
  [Edit...]^c^cddatte
  [<-Extract...]^c^cddattext
[--]
[Filters...]'filter
[Insert...]^c^cddinsert
[Plot...]^c^cplot
```

As explained earlier, $p0=* is the command that makes the cursor pull-down menu appear; it's assigned to Button 2, since it's the first line after ***BUTTONS1 or ***AUX1.

The ***POP1 pull-down menu is a "dummy" pull-down necessary for your cursor menu to work. The name of the cursor menu (in this case, it's [DRAW]) is required under ***POP0, as it is in any other pull-down menu. But because it's only a dummy name that will never appear, it doesn't matter what you put here. Something, however, must go in the name slot in brackets.

Save your TEST2.MNU text file. From AutoCAD, load the menu.

Type: MENU <Enter>

A file dialog box should appear. Find the directory where TEST2.MNU is stored. Now pick TEST2 and OK.

To activate the cursor menu, pick Button 2. The pull-down menu will appear at the crosshairs. (See Figure 7-2.)

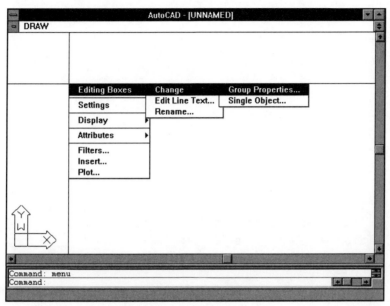

Figure 7-2: Sample cascading cursor menu.

Congratulations! You've just made your first cursor menu. See how easy it is? But it doesn't stop there. Let's revise TEST2.MNU again to create a second cursor menu within the file.

Multiple Cursor Menus

It might seem that if the cursor menu must be ***POP0, you can only have one cursor menu. This is not really so. AutoCAD gives you the ability to load multiple menus into ***POP0. Here's how it's done. Call up TEST2.MNU and modify it as follows:

```
***BUTTONS1
$p0=CURSOR1 $p0=*


***BUTTONS2
$p0=CURSOR2 $p0=*
```

```
***AUX1
$p0=CURSOR1 $p0=*


***AUX2
$p0=CURSOR2 $p0=*


***POP1
[DRAW]
[Line]^c^cline


***POP0
**CURSOR1
[Dialog Boxes]
[->Editing Boxes]
  [->Change]
    [Group Properties...]^c^cddchprop
    [<-Single Object...]^c^cddmodify
  [Edit Line Text...]^c^cddedit
  [<-Rename...]^c^cddrename
[--]
[->Settings]
  [Object Creation...]^c^cddemodes
  [Selection Settings...]^c^cddselect
  [Grips...]^c^cddgrips
  [Layers...]^c^cddlmodes
  [Object Snaps...]^c^cddosnap
  [Points Style...]^c^cddptype
  [Units...]^c^cddunits
  [<-Drawing Aids...]^c^cddrmodes
[--]
[->Display]
  [Views...]^c^cddview
  [->UCS...]
    [UCS Basic...]^c^cdducs
    [<-UCS Right Angle]^c^cdducsp
  [<-Viewpoints...]^c^cddvpoint
```

```
[--]
[->Attributes]
  [Define...]^c^cddattdef
  [Edit...]^c^cddatte
  [<-Extract...]^c^cddattext
[--]
[Filters...]'filter
[Insert...]^c^cddinsert
[Plot...]^c^cplot


**CURSOR2
[DUMMY]
[Line]^c^cline
 [Arc]^c^carc
```

We've added two user sections under ***POP0: **CURSOR1 and **CURSOR2. (Don't forget: user sections have two asterisks, not three.)

There are two BUTTONS sections: ***BUTTONS1 and ***BUTTONS2 or ***AUX1 and ***AUX2. This lets users with only a two-button input device access *both* cursor menus: you'd access **CURSOR1 with Button 2 and **CURSOR2 with Shift+Button 2. When you first modified the TEST2.MNU file to make a cursor menu, the cursor menu line for ***BUTTONS1 or ***AUX1 was simply $p0=*. This brought to the screen the loaded ***POP0, because ***POP0 is always preloaded by default. But now you have *two* sections under ***POP0. Therefore, you'll need to know which section is loaded. Do that with the following line:

```
$p0=CURSOR1
```

This loads **CURSOR1 into the cursor menu. Once loaded, it's brought to the screen with $p0=*. Therefore, $p0=CURSOR1 is assigned to Button 2; then $p0=* brings it to the screen. $p0=CURSOR2 is assigned to Shift+Button 2; then $p0=* brings it to the screen. This way, you can have an unlimited number of cursor menus available.

Save TEST2.MNU with the above changes as a text file. Then load the menu and give it a try.

Menu Rules for Release 13

AutoCAD has attempted to become as consistent as possible with the meaning of its menu structure. Therefore, how you write your menu and what you put after menu names is generally significant. If you observe the following rules, your menus will not only look more like the AutoCAD menus but will also carry more meaning.

- Any screen menu item in all uppercase characters, such as DRAW, has a submenu attached to it.
- Any screen menu item in all uppercase characters and followed by a colon (:), such as LINE:, has a submenu attached to it and automatically cancels any previous command.
- Any menu item followed by three dots (…) calls up a dialog box.
- An item with a right arrowhead after it indicates a cascading menu item attached to the pull-down menu.

Moving On

As you can see, cascading and cursor menus are visually exciting and they help you to be more productive. But AutoCAD's improved visual interest doesn't end there. The next chapter introduces menu graphics. Menus don't have to consist solely of text that flashes across the screen— they can also be graphical.

Image tile menus provide graphical representations of your menu choices, and everybody knows that, unlike machines, humans process pictures faster than words. Chapter 8 teaches you how to create your own image tiles and image tile menus—and with Release 13 they're more visual and easier to use and construct than ever before.

8

Building &
Using Image
Tile Menus

Building & Using Image Tile Menus

What is the most productive yet most underused AutoCAD feature? It has to be image tile menus. What are image tile menus and how do they work? An image tile is a picture on your screen that you can choose by picking. Behind the picture is a menu item, the content of which is whatever you want to make it.

Prior to Release 13, AutoCAD called these menus *icon menus*. With the advent of toolbars with icons, AutoCAD changed the name of the icon menus to *image tile menus*. Even in the AutoCAD menu the ***ICON section has been changed to ***IMAGE. ***ICON will still be recognized through Release 13 to maintain compatibility with previous menus. After Release 13, ***ICON will not be recognized.

The best way to explain image tiles is to show you. From the View pulldown menu choose Tiled Viewports, and then choose Layout. Clearly, it's easier to pick from a picture than it is to learn and remember names.

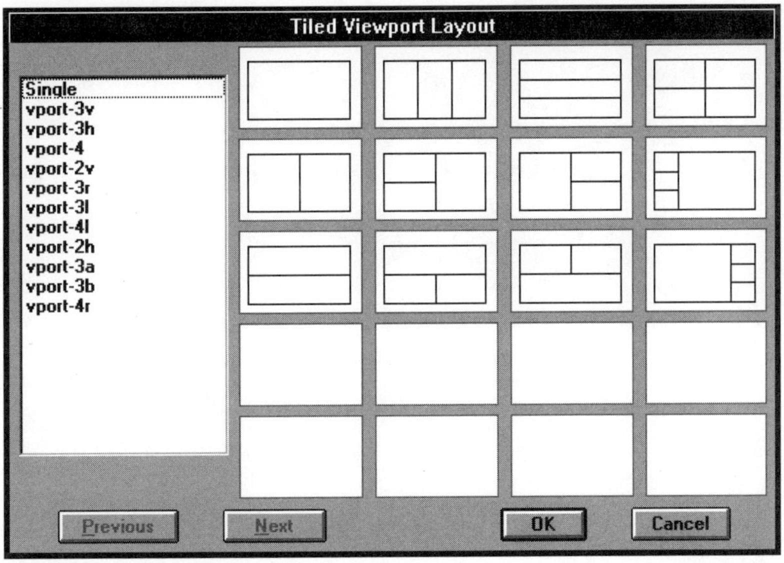

Figure 8-1: Image tile menu.

Beginning with Release 13, AutoCAD has removed most of the image tile menus and changed over to image tiles within dialog boxes. Although dialog boxes are useful and powerful, they are beyond the ability of many users. Therefore image tile menus are still a valuable resource because they provide an easy-to-use graphical representation of blocks to be inserted.

Image tiles can be customized. Because there are several steps to custom-creating image tiles, some people think they're difficult to work with, but nothing could be farther from the truth. If you can work with menus in general, you'll have no trouble working with and creating custom image tile menus.

There are a few basic disadvantages to overcome in working with image tiles in AutoCAD. First, you can't control their size, because AutoCAD automatically sets the size of the image box. Second, you can't control their placement. You can control the order in which they appear but not where they appear on the screen.

Another disadvantage is that the image tiles can't be edited directly, since they're just a series of slides. To change the appearance of an image on a given menu, you must save the original drawing the image slide came from, make the change in the original drawing, and then start from the beginning to compile the slide library.

However, once you get used to working around these problems, you'll want to build more and more image tiles in order to increase your productivity.

Creating & Using an Image Tile Menu

Now let's see how you can make your own image tile menu. This first menu will be simple and easy; it may not be very sophisticated, but it serves as a good learning example.

Begin by creating three images. First, start with a blank drawing, and draw a simple line across the screen, as in Figure 8-2.

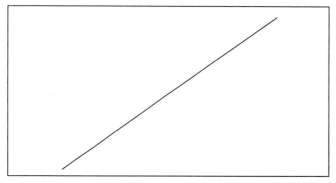

Figure 8-2: A line as a sample image.

Next, make a slide out of this drawing. You may call the slide anything you choose; but to keep it simple, call it LI. This is all you have to do:

Type: MSLIDE <Enter>

A file dialog box will appear again. Enter the name of the slide at the bottom. Call it LI. Make certain you remember the name of the directory in which it is being placed. It is best to make sure the directory is one of your SUPPORT directories so AutoCAD can find the images when the time comes. You probably will use \ACADR13\WIN\SUPPORT.

You now have a slide named LI. Erase the line that's on the screen. Next, draw a circle about the same size as the line you just drew. Be sure that only the circle, not the line, is on the screen. Now make a slide out of the circle:

Type: MSLIDE <Enter>

A file dialog box will appear as before. Enter the name of the slide at the bottom. Call it CI.

You now have a slide named CI. Erase the circle that's on the screen and draw an arc about the same size as the line and the circle you just drew. Be sure that only the arc, not the line or the circle, is on the screen. Now make a slide out of the arc.

Type: MSLIDE <Enter>

A file dialog box will appear. Enter the name of the slide at the bottom. Call it AR.

You now have three slides: LI (a line), CI (a circle) and AR (an arc). The next step is to tell AutoCAD what slides will be used for the image tiles. This is done through an ordinary ASCII text file that you can create with your text editor. The file is called MYIMAGES.TXT, but there's nothing magical about this name; make it anything you choose. The .TXT extension is not required, but it helps identify the file as an ordinary ASCII text file.

Enter the following in your text editor and save the document. Make certain that you place the document in the same directory as the three slides that you have made.

```
LI
CI
AR
```

Making a Slide Library File

The simple file you've just created will act as a data input file for SLIDELIB.EXE, a program supplied by AutoCAD that resides in one of the support directories. Depending on how you installed AutoCAD, it may be in the \ACAD13\COMMON\SUPPORT directory. We'll make that assumption for the rest of the exercise. If the SLIDELIB.EXE file is located elsewhere, substitute the proper directory.

The purpose of SLIDELIB.EXE is to take a series of slides you've created and make them into a single slide library file. But SLIDELIB.EXE must be told what slides you want to use—that's why you created the text file.

To use the SLIDELIB.EXE program, you must be at the operating system or DOS prompt. In Windows the easiest way is to double-click on the MS-DOS Prompt icon, generally found in the Main program group. Shelling out from AutoCAD in Windows to the DOS prompt can be dangerous, so don't use the SHELL command.

At the DOS prompt change to the directory where you placed the text file and the slide files. Then enter the following:

Type: \ACADR13\COMMON\SUPPORT\SLIDELIB MYIMAGES <MYIMAGES.TXT <Enter>

If you get the error message "Bad command or file name," the SLIDELIB program couldn't be found. Make sure you are specifying the proper directory for SLIDELIB.EXE. If necessary, copy that file to your current directory and then leave off the path specification.

If the procedure worked, a copyright notice for SLIDELIB will appear on the screen. Once you have created the library file, exit from the DOS prompt and return to Windows by typing **EXIT** and pressing Enter. In a few seconds, you will have made your first slide library, called MYIMAGES.SLB. (AutoCAD adds the .SLB extension for you.) MYIMAGES.SLB is a single file containing all the slides you will use as image tiles.

Before we move on, let's examine the syntax of the command SLIDELIB MYIMAGES <MYIMAGES.TXT. First of all, SLIDELIB is the executable program provided by AutoCAD. MYIMAGES is the name of the slide library you want the program to create. The < symbol means "take the input from the following file." MYIMAGES.TXT is the name of the file that has the input to be used by SLIDELIB.EXE in order to make MYIMAGES. Remember that MYIMAGES and MYIMAGES.TXT are names we made up. You can call the slide library file anything you want.

Placing Your Image Tile Menu

The next step is to create a place to use the images. The usual choice is the pull-down menus. This is a logical choice, since they pull down in a similar manner. However, it's not the only possibility. Image tile menus can be attached to your mouse button or screen or table menus as well.

Now edit the ACAD.MNU file with your text editor. Search for ***POP5. You will see the first few lines as shown below.

```
***POP5
ID_Options  [&Options]
ID_Dwgaids  [&Drawing Aids...]'_ddrmodes
ID_Osndd    [Running &Object Snap...]'_ddosnap
ID_Cordis   [&Coordinate Display]^D
            [--]
```

After the [--], insert the following line:

```
[My Images]$i=myimages $i=*
```

Your menu should look like this:

```
***POP5
ID_Options  [&Options]
ID_Dwgaids  [&Drawing Aids...]'_ddrmodes
ID_Osndd    [Running &Object Snap...]'_ddosnap
ID_Cordis   [&Coordinate Display]^D
            [--]
[My Images]$i=myimages $i=*
```

The rest of the ***POP5 menu lines then follow. Make sure that you do not have any blank lines within the menu section itself.

All you've done with the line above, [My Images]$i=myimages $i=*, is to call up your image tile menu and make it appear on your screen. This is not where you define what you want the individual image tiles to do. That comes next. Look at what you just entered as a menu item:

```
[My Images]$i=myimages $i=*
```

Just as $S= calls up screen menu items and $P1= calls up pull-down menu items, $I= calls up image tile menu items. And just as the $P1=

command loads the pull-down menu information into pull-down menu
Area 1, and $P1=* pulls down the menu, $I= loads the image tile menu
information, and $I=* pulls down the image tile menu.

```
$i=myimages
```

This is a menu section like any other menu section. It will begin with
**myimages, and you select a name for it. Although in this example
you've used the name MYIMAGES for the .TXT file and the .SLB file, as
well as the name **myimages for the submenu section, this has been done
only as a matter of convenience. These names don't have to be identical.
It's just easier, when you're creating the files and the menu sections, to
give them the same or similar names in order to keep them straight. You
can name them anything you want.

The final step is to find a place to put **myimages. This section can't be
placed just anywhere in the ACAD.MNU file. It belongs in a special
section called ***image.

Search for ***image in your file. You should see the following:

```
***image
**image_poly
[Set Spline Fit Variables]
[acad(pm-quad,Quadric Fit Mesh)]'_surftype 5
[acad(pm-cubic,Cubic Fit Mesh)]'_surftype 6
[acad(pm-bezr,Bezier Fit Mesh)]'_surftype 8
[acad(pl-quad,Quadric Fit Pline)]'_splinetype 5
[acad(pl-cubic,Cubic Fit Pline)]'_splinetype 6

**image_3DObjects
[3D Objects]
```

Place your menu before **image_3DObjects. The only important thing
that you have to concern yourself with is that there be one blank line
between the end of your section and the beginning of the next section.

Insert the following:

```
**myimages
[THESE ARE MY OWN IMAGES]
[MYIMAGES(LI)]^C^Cline
```

```
[MYIMAGES(CI)]^C^Ccircle
[MYIMAGES(AR)]^C^Carc
```

Save your menu file and exit the text editor. Now load the AutoCAD menu.

Accessing Your Menu

Do you remember where your slides are? They're in the file called MYIMAGES.SLB. You placed them there in a certain order using the SLIDELIB.EXE program. Since all the slides are in a single file, they're no longer called LI, CI and AR (the names you gave when you created them). You access these slides with the name of the slide file and a subscript that stands for the name of the slide. Therefore, MYIMAGES(LI) is the line; MYIMAGES(CI) is the circle and MYIMAGES(AR) is the arc. Notice that each of these is in brackets on the screen. To the right of the brackets is what you want the image to do when it's picked, the same as with any other menu item we've created thus far.

Let's try out our new image tiles. Go to your pull-down menus and pick Options. Pick My Images from the entries. When your image tiles come down, pick any one of the three, and you'll be in the LINE, CIRCLE or ARC command. (See Figure 8-3.)

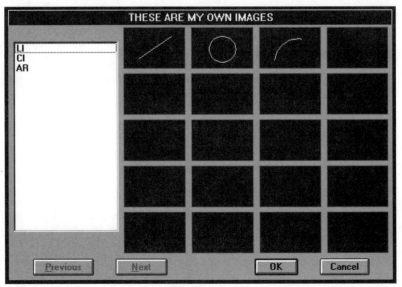

Figure 8-3: Your new image tile menu.

You'll notice that the images don't have little boxes next to them; in this version you pick the image itself. Also, there's a list scroll box to the left of the image tiles. Pick the words in the scroll box, and the image lights up; pick the image, and the words light up. A double-click will activate the image; so will picking the image and then OK.

Note that there's something wrong with our list box. You don't really want the list box to say LI, CI and AR, do you? It got these names from the names of the slides. If the slides had been named LINE, CIRCLE and ARC, the names would automatically appear. But you can force any wording you want, up to 17 letters, in the list box. Here's how you do it.

Modify the **myimages section of your ACAD.MNU file as follows:

```
***image
**myimages
[THESE ARE MY OWN IMAGES]
[MYIMAGES(LI,Line)]^C^Cline
[MYIMAGES(CI,Circle)]^C^Ccircle
[MYIMAGES(AR,Arc)]^C^Carc
```

Save the ACAD.MNU text file and reload your menu. Notice now that the words Line, Circle and Arc appear.

Trouble-Shooting

If your image tile menu didn't work, here are some things that could have gone wrong:

- When you picked the Options item from the menu bar, My Images was there but the rest of the Options menu was gone.

  ANSWER: You added a blank line after My Images. Remember, a blank line tells AutoCAD that a pull-down menu is complete. Remove the blank line, and the rest of the menu will appear.

- When you picked the My Images item, nothing happened.

  ANSWER: You may have misspelled $i=myimages, or the **myimages section doesn't have the exact same name. Another possibility is that you didn't place the **myimages section in the ***image section. A third possibility is that you left out the $i=*, the command that pulls down the image tile menu. AutoCAD won't pull down the menu without this command, even if it's loaded.

- The image screen pulled down, but no images appeared in the squares. Yet when you picked the squares, they did what they're supposed to do.

  ANSWER: You didn't correctly spell the name of the slide file, or you didn't create a slide file by this name. An easy mistake to make is to confuse the ( ) with the [ ]. Each line must read exactly as follows: [MYIMAGES(LI)].

- The words MYIMAGES(LI) appeared on the image screen, but not the image tiles themselves.

  ANSWER: You put a space before the word [MYIMAGES(LI)]. Remember that this is AutoCAD's way of knowing the difference between a slide file and just a word. If there's a space, AutoCAD thinks it's not a slide file.

Tips & Tricks

Here are a few suggestions that will help you work with image tiles:

- When you're creating the slides for the image tiles, it's important to get the size of the drawings consistent, so you don't have a big circle in one of the image tiles and a little arc in another. An easy way to do this is to ZOOM EXTENTS, then ZOOM .9X before you create the slide. This will give each slide the same general size.

- The images we created in this exercise are not very attractive. But since an image tile is nothing more than a slide, you can dress it up and make it as colorful as you want. Remember also that a slide is nothing but the raster image at the time you made the slide. If you normally have a black background, you might want to change that to a light background just for the slide. This can be done through Preferences from the Options menu. So if you want your image tiles to be colorful, make them colorful as you create them.

- It's also a good idea to add text to the images. Place whatever text you want below or to the side of the image in the drawing itself. Then when you make the slide, the text will be included. This is the only way to add instructions.

- If you need to change the appearance of an image tile, call up the original drawing and make your change. Then save it under the same slide name. You'll have to redo the slide file, so save *all* the original drawings in case you need to make changes. If you don't save all the original slides, you'll have to make each one of them over again from the drawing files. You can't add just one slide to the entire slide file. But you don't have to redo the text file that acted as the input file for SLIDELIB.EXE.

- You might have wondered why you need to make a slide file. Can't the image tile menu access the slide directly? The answer is yes. Instead of the first line below you could have placed the second line:

```
[MYIMAGES(LI,Line)]^c^cline
[LI,Line]^c^cline
```

However, there's a major problem with doing it this way. If you ever optimize your disk and the individual slide files end up in different sectors, bringing up your images will take a very long time. If all of the slides are in a single file, the images will come up rapidly, because AutoCAD doesn't have to search all over the disk to find the slides.

How to Use Image Tile Menus

There's no one best way to use image tile menus. You can use them in just about any way that serves your purpose. One of the most practical uses is in accessing your detail parts library. Here's a way you might consider.

Let's assume that you have 12 similar items, such as machine screws. Create a MACHINE SCREWS icon on one of your toolbars. (You'll learn how to do this in Chapter 9.) Then when you pick the MACHINE SCREWS icon on the toolbar, the 12 image tiles of machine screws pull down on your screen.

As you might have figured out by now, the pull-down menu area isn't always the ideal place to put image tile menus. In fact, it can be the worst place, because the pull-down menu area is already crowded. The following is what you would enter on the executable line of the toolbar icon. The icon button is really not a menu and therefore it requires that the image tile menu be accessed through AutoLISP.

```
(menucmd "i=myimages")(menucmd "i=*")
```

Recap

Let's take a final look at the steps necessary to create image tile menus:

1. Create images on the screen.
2. Use MSLIDE to make individual slides.
3. Create a text file with names of the slides.
4. Use the SLIDELIB command to create a slide library file.
5. Create access to images in the .MNU file (generally in one of the POP menu areas).
6. Add image tiles to ***IMAGE section of .MNU file. Now your image tiles are ready to use.

Moving On

Image tile menus are extremely valuable. Give them a try. It may seem like a lot of steps to go through at first, but once you've done a few menus, it becomes almost automatic. I hope you'll persevere—the increase in your productivity will make it well worth the effort.

In the next chapter, we'll take a look at another major element of the AutoCAD menu system, and perhaps the most exciting interface improvement in Release 13: customizable toolbars. Autodesk has made these important time-savers easy to use, modify and create.

9

Customizing Toolbars

Customizing Toolbars

The most exciting interface improvement in Release 13 is undoubtedly the advent of customizable toolbars. Autodesk has made these important tools easy to use, modify and create. Let's begin by taking a look at what a toolbar is. See Figure 9-1 for an example of the Draw toolbar.

Figure 9-1: Draw toolbar.

A toolbar is made up of a series of buttons known as icons. There are two types of icons: regular single-pick icons and flyout icons. The single-pick icons are the simplest. When you pick them the command occurs. The single-pick icons do not have an arrow in the lower right of the icon. Flyout icons let you group icons on toolbars, giving you access to more icons than would be possible if each of the icons were a single command. See Figure 9-2 for an example of flyout icons.

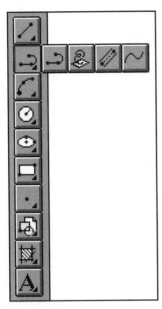

Figure 9-2: Flyout icons.

Figure 9-2 shows the Polyline flyout. You know it is a flyout because of the downward arrow at the lower right corner of the icon. A flyout is activated by picking and holding down the pick button. The flyout then exposes the other icons. With the pick button depressed, drag the arrow over the other icons until you get to the icon you want to pick, then release the pick button. As you drag the arrow and pause over any icon, the name or tooltip of the icon appears. (See Figure 9-3.)

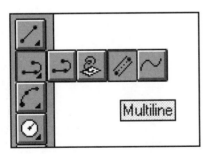

Figure 9-3: Name or tooltip of icon.

Because the size of the name is limited, AutoCAD also provides a help message for each icon. The help message appears at the status line as you pass over and pause at an icon. (See Figure 9-4.)

Figure 9-4: The help message for the Multiline icon on the Draw toolbar.

Modifying Existing Toolbars

There are two ways to modify an existing toolbar. You can modify the properties and commands of an existing icon on the toolbar, or you can add or delete an icon on a toolbar. Let's look at the first scenario. We will simply change the command information on an existing icon.

To begin any editing scenario, right-click on any icon. It doesn't have to be the icon you want to change, although you will save a step if it is. In this example we are going to right-click on the Polyline icon on the Draw toolbar. This will bring up the Toolbars dialog box. (See Figure 9-5.)

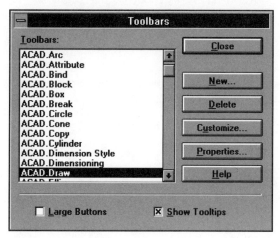

Figure 9-5: Toolbars dialog box.

The available toolbars are listed in the Toolbars list box. The toolbar that you right-clicked on is highlighted. In Figure 9-5, ACAD.Draw is highlighted because we right-clicked on an icon on the Draw toolbar. If the highlighted toolbar isn't the one you wish to change, pick a different toolbar name from the list box.

While on this dialog box, let's look at some of the component parts. The Toolbars list box shows all of the toolbars that are available to you. They are divided in what are known as menu groups. Each menu that is loaded should have a menu group. If you remember, this is a major menu section that begins the menu such as ***MENUGROUP= followed by the name of the menu group. When toolbars are saved, they are saved to the menu that is designated by the menu group. Multiple menus and menu groups are loaded as a base menu plus partial loadable menus. (See Chapter 10 for more about partial loadable menus.) In our examples each of the toolbars belongs to the ACAD menu group. (The menu group name is to the left of the period.)

At the bottom of the dialog box are two check boxes. The one on the left permits you to have icons that are twice the size of the regular icons. They should generally be used only if you are using an extremely high resolution, such as 1600 x 1240. In this case the smaller icons may be too small to read. The other check box turns tooltips on or off. (A tooltip is the short name of an icon, as illustrated in Figure 9-3.)

On the right of the dialog box is a series of buttons. Pick the Properties button, and the Toolbar Properties dialog box appears. (See Figure 9-6.)

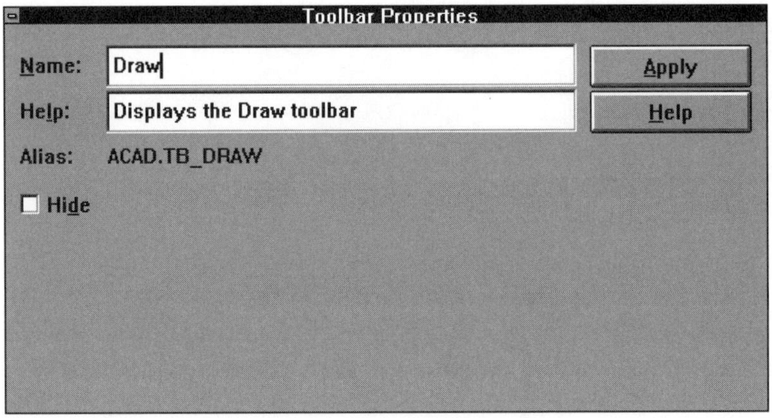

Figure 9-6: Toolbar Properties dialog box.

The Toolbar Properties dialog box permits you to change the name of the toolbar as well as change the help message that appears at the status line.

From the Toolbars dialog box shown in Figure 9-5, you can also pick the Delete button. This will delete the toolbar from your menu file. If you do this then you cannot bring the toolbar up again unless you recreate it from scratch. You can also pick the New button, which will give you the ability to create a new toolbar. We'll get to that one later. For now let's concentrate on the Customize button and how it works.

Before you pick the Customize button it's important to have the entire flyout on the screen, if this is a flyout icon. In this case we want to show you where you can change the Polyline icon on the Draw toolbar. If you're working with a flyout you will not be able to pick the Polyline icon by itself unless you isolate the entire flyout. To do this, pick the Polyline flyout with your pick button. When you do this the flyout shows up on the screen as an isolated toolbar. (See Figure 9-7.)

Figure 9-7: Isolated Polyline flyout on Draw toolbar.

To change the command or properties of an existing button it's not necessary to pick the Customize button. You only need to do that if you're adding or deleting buttons. For now all you have to do is right-click on the button you want to change. In this case it's the Polyline icon on the isolated Polyline flyout. You'll now see the Button Properties dialog box. (See Figure 9-8.)

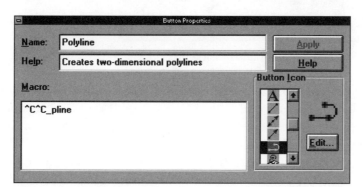

Figure 9-8: Button Properties dialog box.

In this dialog box you can change the name of the icon. This is also the tooltip. The help information is listed in the Help text box. The Macro text box is where the real action takes place. In our example it is listed as

^C^C_pline. Here you can customize the macro to anything you wish, including AutoLISP commands and programs. If you don't like the picture of the icon, you can change it to one of the existing icons in the Button Icon list box. This is a list of standard icons you can choose from. Or you can redesign or load another icon by pressing the Edit button next to the Button Icon list scroll bar. Once all changes are made, pick the Apply button and your changes will be applied to the icon. When you are finished, double-click on the close box at the upper left-hand corner.

Adding Icons

You can also add icons to an existing toolbar. Here's how that's done. Begin as before in the Toolbars dialog box as shown in Figure 9-5. Make sure that you have isolated the flyout to which you want to add an icon. If you simply want to add an icon to the basic toolbar itself, this step is not necessary. From the list box pick the toolbar that you want to edit and then pick Customize. The dialog box shown in Figure 9-9 appears.

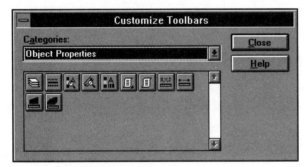

Figure 9-9: Customize Toolbars dialog box.

From the Categories drop box you can choose any of the standard areas such as Draw, Modify and Object Properties. If you choose icons from this area you may also choose to use and inherit their normal commands. For example, if you pick the Draw buttons and then the Line button, the icon will come ready-made with the LINE command. That doesn't mean that you can't initially use the Line button as an icon and then modify the accompanying command later and even make a change to the appearance of the icon itself.

When you have chosen the icon, pick the icon, hold down the pick button and drag it into place onto the toolbar. It's as simple as that. If you want to delete an icon from the toolbar, pick the icon on the toolbar, hold down the pick button and drag it back to the Customize Toolbars dialog box. It will then be removed from the toolbar.

If you don't want to use any of the existing icon buttons, choose Custom from the drop box. Here you will see two buttons, as illustrated in Figure 9-10.

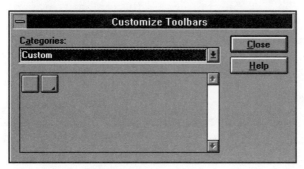

Figure 9-10: Custom buttons.

Here the two buttons are blank. The one on the left is a regular single-pick button and the one on the right is a flyout. If you drag either of these buttons to the toolbar they will be added. Once the blank buttons are added, right-click on one of the blank buttons and edit the icon information, including an icon picture. Then pick Apply.

If the blank button is a flyout there is an extra step. You first must create a new toolbar to hold the additional buttons. (See the next section for more on creating a new toolbar.) Add the appropriate buttons to the new toolbar. Now come back to the blank flyout button and right-click. This will give you the Flyout Properties dialog box. Add the name of the flyout and the help information. Generally you are not going to add an icon here. You'll generally want to pick up the icon of the button you used most recently. (See Figure 9-11.)

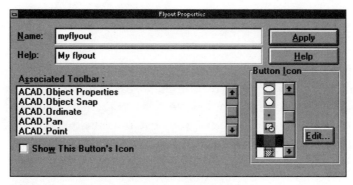

Figure 9-11: Flyout Properties dialog box.

The important thing here is to pick from the Associated Toolbar list box the new toolbar that you have created. That will then associate that toolbar as the flyout for your new flyout button. Remember to pick Apply and close all dialog boxes. Your new flyout is now ready to go. The confusing part here is that the associated toolbar is the toolbar you want to fly out. It is not the toolbar on which the flyout belongs. That is determined by dragging the initial button to the appropriate toolbar.

Creating New Toolbars

To create a new toolbar, move your pick arrow over any icon and right-click. The Toolbars dialog box appears as shown in Figure 9-5. Now pick New, and the New Toolbar dialog box appears. (See Figure 9-12.)

Figure 9-12: New Toolbar dialog box.

Enter in the name of the new toolbar in the Toolbar Name text box. Notice that the Menu Group defaults to ACAD. Therefore in our example the name of the new toolbar is ACAD.NEWTOOL. To assign the toolbar to a different menu group, pick the drop arrow and then pick a menu group from the list that appears. When you are finished, pick OK. At this point the toolbar has been created and you will see it on the screen. You can add icons to the toolbar now or later.

Editing an Icon

To edit an icon, move the pick arrow over the icon and right-click. The Toolbars dialog box appears. Right-click again on the same icon. (This assumes that the icon is a single-level icon. If the icon is part of a flyout, pick once on the flyout to expose the nested icons, then right-click on the icon you want to change.) The Button Properties dialog box appears. Now pick Edit. The Button Editor dialog box appears, as shown in Figure 9-13.

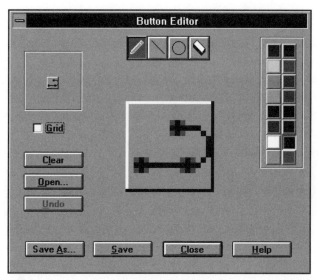

Figure 9-13: Button Editor dialog box.

Here you can modify or paint a new icon using the pen, line, circle and erasure features along with a color palette. You can also check the Grid check box and turn a pixel grid on to help you.

When the icon is as you like it, pick Save. If you think you would like to use this icon again, pick Save As. Now give it a file name and pick OK. When you are finished, pick Close to close the dialog box. Then pick Apply to place the icon on the button that you have chosen. The icon is saved as a .BMP file.

You are not limited to the icons that AutoCAD has created for you. You can also use icons that you have created independently through another program. Use any program that creates a .BMP file, such as Paintbrush. When you have created the icon, return to AutoCAD and access the Button Editor as described above. Pick the Open button and choose to bring in the .BMP file that you created. Watch out for the scale at which you created the original, because you begin to lose detail when the original is above 100 x 100 pixels (pels) in Paintbrush language. AutoCAD uses 16 x 16 for small buttons and 32 x 32 for large buttons.

Moving On

 With the onslaught of third-party software and the increasing number of Autodesk programs, the competition for ACAD.MNU has been fierce. In the past the loser has been the AutoCAD user. The loadable partial pull-down menu is the answer. As you will learn in the next chapter, this innovation lets any developer add custom pull-down menus to the base menu without interference. In this way all menus can work together. It adds a bonus to the user in that they are easy to create and maintain.

10

Loadable Partial Pull-Down Menus

Loadable Partial Pull-Down Menus

For years Autodesk has had a problem with competition from third-party AutoCAD menu programs. In the past, each third-party software vendor began with the basic ACAD.MNU file and modified it by either adding to it or rearranging its parts. The vendor may have left it as ACAD.MNU or changed its name.

If you were using only one third-party application, this generally worked out okay. The rub came if you were using more than one third-party application. In this event each application wanted you to use its menu. This problem came to a head when Autodesk began releasing a plethora of new programs at the same time. These included AutoVision, ADE, AutoSurf and Designer. Each one of these new programs wanted its own ACAD.MNU. This chaos gave rise to the advent of the loadable partial pull-down menu.

You don't have to be a third-party programmer to take advantage of these menus. Their ease of creation and use make them the ideal way for the average AutoCAD user to create custom pull-down menus. Everything that you have learned thus far is applicable to the loadable pull-downs. What makes them easy to work with is that you don't have to go into the ACAD.MNU file itself in order to create and use these menus. This means that you can create and use your own pull-downs as separate files and load them as you need them.

Release 13 gives you the ability to write your own pull-down menus totally apart from the main base menu. These menus are loadable on demand and remain as part of the menu system as long as you are in AutoCAD, even between drawings. Prior to Release 13 AutoCAD reloaded the menu each time you loaded a new or existing drawing. Now the menu stays constant unless the new drawing loads a different base menu. The basic rules for creating a pull-down menu still apply. This includes separators. ***POP1, and cascading menus. What is different here is what you have to do to make sure that Release 13 recognizes your pull-down menu as loadable. There are two things that distinguish a loadable menu from a base menu: it must define a menu group using the ***MENUGROUP section, and it must be in its own file—*not* the same file as the base menu.

Begin with a text editor and create a text file with a single pull-down menu. The file should carry the extension .MNU. The following is an example of the minimum necessary for a loadable pull-down menu.

```
***MENUGROUP=AMECH
***POP1
[/MECH]
[->/MMM Conversions]
  [/CCircle]^c^camcimm
  [/DDiameter]^c^camdimm
  [/iDistance]^c^camdismm
```

The menu must begin with ***MENUGROUP= as the first line. This permits you to give a unique name to the menu group, which will be needed to load the menu. This is followed by a ***POP and a number. Unlike a regular pull-down menu section within the traditional base menu, this doesn't mean that the menu must appear in the first location when it is loaded. It may be inserted and placed within any location. But a POP number must be available. If there is only one pull-down within the file, begin it with 1.

Traditionally the first line of the pull-down is what will appear in the menu bar. This is true of the loadable pull-down menu. The rest of the menu is the same as any other pull-down menu. It follows all of the same rules. The above is the minimum necessary to create a loadable pull down menu. The first time it is used the .MNU file will be converted to an .MNS file and then be compiled to an .MNC file.

Loading a Loadable Partial Pull-Down Menu

As you can see, the creation of a loadable partial pull-down menu is basically the same as creating any POP pull-down menu in the main base menu. In this case the loadable pull-down must have its own ***MENU-GROUP section. It must not conflict with the name of any other menu group that is going to be loaded. After that the ***POP section is the same. This includes cascading menus. There is no reason why you can't have more than one POP section within a single file.

Begin with the assumption that the name of the menu file you are using is MECH.MNU. The name of the menu group is AMECH and the name of the POP1 pull-down menu is just MECH. Each of these names is different so that you can see the difference and the relationship of the component parts.

Pick Customize Menus from the Tools menu or enter **MENULOAD** from the command line. (See Figure 10-1.)

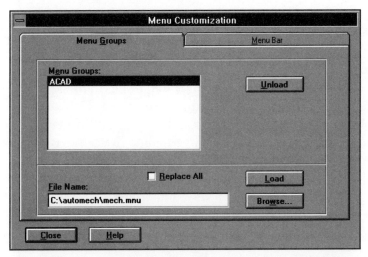

Figure 10-1: The Menu Groups page of the Menu Customization dialog box.

Using the Browse button find the menu that you want to load, or type in the complete file and path specification for the menu. Now pick Load. The name of the menu group should now appear in the Menu Groups list box. Now pick Menu Bar at the top of the dialog box. This lets you place the pull-down menu on your menu bar. (See Figure 10-2.)

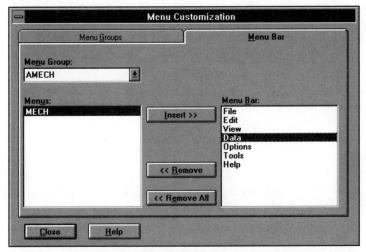

Figure 10-2: The Menu Bar page of the Menu Customization dialog box.

From the Menu Group list box pick the drop arrow and pick AMECH. In the Menus list box is a list of the available POP or pull-down menus for the AMECH group. In this case there is only one: MECH. Highlight MECH and pick Insert>>. Now pick the Close button to close the dialog box. The menu will now be added to the menu bar. In fact you'll see it being added as you pick the Insert button.

To place this menu on your menu bar at a specific location, begin by picking and highlighting the pull-down menu in the Menu Bar list box where you want your new menu to be inserted. That's the list box on the right in Figure 10-2. Now pick Insert>>. The pull-down will be added at that location and you'll see it immediately on your existing menu bar. If you want to change the position, the easiest way is to highlight the menu in the menu bar list box and pick <<Remove. This will place it on the other side. Now pick the pull-down menu in the Menu Bar list box where you want your menu to be inserted before and pick Insert>>. It will now be repositioned.

Removing Pull-Down Menus

There are two ways to remove a pull-down menu from the menu bar. The first is as mentioned above. Highlight the menu that you want to remove in the Menu Bar list box on the Menu Bar page of the Menu Customization dialog box, then pick the <<Remove button. The menu will move to the left side and will disappear from the menu bar immediately.

You may want to remove the entire menu group. That is done by unloading the group. When a group is unloaded, then all of the individual pull-down menus are also removed. Pick Customize Menus from the Tools menu or enter **MENULOAD** from the command line. Pick the menu group that you want to unload and then pick the Unload button (shown in Figure 10-1). The group and all the pull-downs in the group will be removed.

The Base Menu

You shouldn't use just loadable pull-down menus by themselves. You generally will have what is known as a base or template menu. Loadable pull-down menus are added to the base menu. The base menu is determined by the regular AutoCAD MENU command. Pick the menu as you have always done. This becomes your base menu. Now you can add other loadable pull-down menus.

Maintaining Loadable Pull-Downs

One of the biggest problems with loadable partial pull-down menus is that they are not saved with the current drawing, nor are they recognized in any configuration file. This can be a problem since you would have to go through the above steps every time you started AutoCAD.

If you want the custom menus loaded each time you enter AutoCAD, you'll need to write an AutoLISP program and place it in your S::STARTUP function of your ACAD.LSP file. Here is an example of how that can be done. Again this assumes that the name of the menu file is MECH.MNU. The name of the group is AMECH and the pull-down menu that you are loading into the fifth position is POP1.

```
(defun s::startup ( )
  (setq fid (getvar "filedia"))
  (setvar "filedia" 0)
  (command "menuunload" "amech")
  (command "menuload" "mech")
  (menucmd "p5=+amech.pop1")
  ( setvar "filedia" fid)
)
```

This file begins by saving the system variable FILEDIA and setting FILEDIA to 0. In order to use this file the system variable FILEDIA must be set to 0 so that a file dialog box does not come up. The program next unloads the existing menu group AMECH if it is loaded. This is because you can't load twice.

Now you will load the file. Notice that you *unload* the group, but you *load* the file. As long as the menu file is in the AutoCAD support directory, you don't need to give it a path specification. If it were not, you would have to tell the program where to find the file. Remember that when you're using AutoLISP, directories are divided using the forward slash (/), not the backslash (\).

Using the (menucmd) AutoLISP function, p5 sets the position on the menu bar. This places the menu in the fifth position on the menu bar. The + sign in front of amech.pop1 says insert. If you wanted to remove the menu from the menu bar you would use a - sign. Notice that POP1 is specified as AMECH.POP1, which is its real name within the menu group, since you can have several loadable menus all called POP1. AMECH is the name of the menu group. Finally set the FILEDIA system variable back to the way it was.

This looks like a lot of trouble, but at present is the only way to assure that the menu is always available without having to load it manually.

Moving On

Loadable partial pull-down menus are quite an advancement in menu creation. They give you the convenience of working within your own small file, but also the ability to move your own menus to any menu system in effect, whether it is a third-party system or someone else's custom menu. It also protects your investment in menu construction from changes as updates of AutoCAD come out.

You've learned in the last few chapters how to create your own menus—screen menus, pull-down menus, tablet menus, button menus, accelerator keys, toolbars—as well as how to use loadable partial pull-down menus. You gain productivity by making each of these menus work together, not just by themselves. The next chapter helps you look beyond simply building a menu to creating a complete system where one menu can work in cooperation with others.

11

Using
Multiple
Menu
Systems

Using Multiple Menu Systems

Have you ever noticed that when you pick the LINE command from the tablet menu, the screen menu with the other options is activated? Using a tablet menu to activate a screen menu in order to provide more menu areas is one example of how AutoCAD compensates for certain limitations. You're given the appropriate screen menu for each tablet menu item you choose.

You should focus on this type of capability when planning your own customized menus. It isn't enough just to create a series of menus; your menus must work together. It's the relationships between the menus you've created and the tasks that need to be done that bring about real productivity. The technology is only as valuable as you make it.

How you go about making your menus work together depends on what you are trying to accomplish. In this chapter we'll take a look at which types of menus and input methods are best suited to the typical AutoCAD tasks and activities. We'll also learn how to program function keys and accelerator keys, as well as how to make one menu call another and how to call a menu from AutoLISP.

The Basic Tools

When working with AutoCAD, there are four basic things that you can get menus and other input methods to do for you:

- Issue AutoCAD commands
- Run AutoLISP programs
- Insert blocks
- Control your drawing aids

AutoCAD commands include the basic commands, such as LINE, ARC, PEDIT and ERASE, and the subcommands. For example, the DVIEW command has as many as 12 options. PEDIT also has several options. With virtually every AutoCAD command, options follow the initial command.

AutoLISP programs are specialized programs designed to accomplish specific tasks. If you know AutoLISP, you write these yourself or have someone else write them for you. You can find many efficient and productive AutoLISP programs in computer magazines, bulletin boards and books, at no cost to you. There are 30 ready-to-run programs included with this book, more than 100 ready-to-use AutoLISP programs in *1000 AutoCAD Tips & Tricks* and still more in *AutoCAD 3D Companion* (both from Ventana Press). The point is, you don't have to look far to find AutoLISP programs to help you work more efficiently. There are also third-party commercial programs for your particular discipline that are basically a series of AutoLISP programs or sometimes AutoLISP and ADS (Auto-CAD Development System) combined.

Inserting blocks is one of the most powerful things that menus can do for you. All you have to do is pick the insertion point and the menu controls everything else.

Drawing aids are things like Snap, Grid and Ortho On and Off, various Object Snaps and many other commands that can be made transparent within an AutoCAD command, including AutoLISP programming.

The following table shows the various menus and other input methods that you can use to select the functions and activities described above. Any of these input methods can be used to access any of the types of activities, but some input methods are more suited to certain types of commands and functions (though that is not to say that, in certain situations, other input methods can't or shouldn't be used).

Input Method	Typically Used For
Screen menus	AutoCAD commands
Pull-down menus	AutoLISP programs
Tablet menus	AutoCAD commands, inserting blocks, AutoLISP programs
Digitizer puck/mouse buttons	Drawing aids
Image tile menus	Inserting blocks
Toolbars	Everything
Keyboard entry	Everything
Function keys	Drawing aids
Accelerator keys	Drawing aids
Dialog boxes	Drawing aids, inserting blocks, multiple choices, saving and importing files

Let's take a closer look at some of the most common and efficient input methods used for each of the four basic types of AutoCAD activity.

AutoCAD Commands

AutoCAD commands are best handled through toolbars or through the keyboard. The keyboard is a viable option if you can develop a series of quick one- and two-keystroke abbreviations for each common AutoCAD command or a series of accelerator keys. Whenever you're dealing with subcommands, AutoCAD always lets you use one- and two-letter abbreviations. When using the PEDIT command, for example, most users find it's easier to enter the letter J for JOIN than to pick JOIN from the screen menu. But, when you pick PEDIT from a tablet, screen or pull-down menu, as well as selected toolbar flyouts, you also get a side screen of options to pick from, or are taken to the specific subcommand directly. Typically, pull-down menus aren't nearly as efficient as toolbars or single-key abbreviations and accelerator keys. Screen menus are probably the least efficient method of input because of their multiple nesting. If you're not careful, pull-down menus can inherit this problem as well.

AutoLISP Programs

You can efficiently place AutoLISP programs on any of the menus and input methods, but they are best suited to pull-down menus, toolbars and keyboard input. AutoLISP programs work best when commands can be reduced to two-keystroke abbreviations or placed on toolbars. If there are large numbers of these programs, they must be organized in a special way. If you place 50 to 100 AutoLISP programs on toolbars it is difficult to differentiate what's what. Here it is probably best to use pull-downs organized in groups depending on what tasks the AutoLISP programs are to do. Combine this with a simple toolbar for the most used AutoLISP programs. Depending on how many programs and groups you're working with, it is possible to make toolbars more efficient by creating flyouts. But when too many programs and groups are involved, pull-downs are still the most efficient mechanism. Don't fall into the trap of trying to make flyouts of flyouts.

Grouping may seem like an extra step, but in the long run it's more productive. With so many blocks and AutoLISP programs, a user typically spends too much time trying to find all but the most frequently used AutoLISP programs. But with grouping, just two quick picks guide you directly to the proper choice. If you use a command so often that it's become automatic, take advantage of its two-character counterpart command if one was written in—it's quicker to type.

Inserting Blocks

This is generally done through an AutoLISP line. For example assume that the name of the block is PART1. The following is a sample AutoLISP line that can be placed in your menu to insert it.

```
(command "insert" "part1" pause "1" "1" "0")
```

You should rarely need the INSERT command if you've done your job right and created a productive menu system. To insert a part into your drawing, there's no reason you should have to pick INSERT, then try to remember the name of the right block. If it's important enough to make a block out of, it's important enough to place on a menu with all the commands necessary to insert it into a drawing. This is where special toolbar buttons combined with image tile menus are handy. The image tile menu gives you the ability to see what the block looks like and pick from the picture, and you can have a toolbar icon activate the image tile menu.

Drawing Aids

Drawing aids must be available while you're in an AutoCAD command. Object Snaps are a prime example: While you're in a LINE command, you must be able to issue Int, Endp, Mid, Cen, etc. The cursor menu is one efficient way. Use it. This is achieved by activating the third (or Shift+second) button of the mouse when you're in a command. Other minor drawing aids can also be controlled through menus, such as the UCS and the UCS icon.

Programming Function Keys

Function keys have a very special use. Because the number of function keys available is limited, they should be reserved for transparent commands only. AutoCAD supports direct programming of function keys in two ways: conventional programming, which works only in DOS, and accelerator key programming, which works only in AutoCAD for Windows. This section describes the conventional method. The accelerator key method is discussed later in the chapter.

In order to reprogram the function keys using the conventional method, you must have the following statement in the root directory in a text file called CONFIG.SYS:

```
device=ansi.sys
```

ANSI.SYS is a device driver furnished on your DOS disk. Make sure this file is copied to your root directory. It can be in another directory (such as DOS); if so, though, in order to path spec directly to the file, the CONFIG.SYS file must read DEVICE=\DOS\ANSI.SYS. You can set up or check the CONFIG.SYS file from inside AutoCAD. In fact, it may already be set up and active.

If the ANSI.SYS driver was not active before, and you made the change to the CONFIG.SYS file, you will have to reboot your computer before you can use it. Once ANSI.SYS is set up, you can enter ANSI codes to reprogram virtually any key on your keyboard. The model for all key redirection is as follows:

```
ESC[0;62;'int,end';13p
```

0;62 is the keyboard code for F4. 'int,endp' is what you want it to say when you press F4. 13 is the code for a carriage return. All of these codes must begin with ESC and end with p.

The only problem is that ESC can't be entered this way, nor can it be entered with the Esc key on your keyboard. There are three ways that the function keys can be reprogrammed: with BASIC programs, AutoLISP programs and batch files. The three methods are covered in the sections that follow.

BASIC Programs

The first way to assign a function key is to create a small program in BASIC and run the program before you go into AutoCAD. The program should have only one line for each of the keys you're reprogramming. Here is the BASIC program listing:

```
10 print chr$(27)+"[0;62;'int,endp';13p"
```

AutoLISP Programs

You can create a similar program in AutoLISP. To make certain the function keys are activated when you enter the drawing editor, you might want to put the program in the S::STARTUP function of the ACAD.LSP file. Here is the AutoLISP program listing:

```
(defun S::STARTUP ()
    (textscr)
    (prompt "\e[0;62;'int,endp';13p")
    (graphscr)
)
```

Batch Files

You can also activate the function keys from the AUTOEXEC.BAT file or from a special batch file. The following statements would be placed in the batch file:

```
prompt $e[0;62;'int,endp';13p
prompt $p$g
```

If you're using a batch file, it's very important that you end the batch with the prompt pg, or whatever prompt you're using, because the prompt statement that sets the function keys also unsets your traditional prompt statement. If you leave it this way without the final prompt pg, you won't have a prompt at all. It will just be a blank line with a blinking cursor.

Function Key Codes

In each of the examples above, we've used 0;62, the code for the F4 key. The following is a complete list of the codes you can use for all the function keys; Alt function keys and Alt with any other key; and Ctrl function keys and Ctrl with any other key.

Keyboard Code	Function Key
0;59	F1
0;60	F2
0;61	F3
0;62	F4
0;63	F5
0;64	F6
0;65	F7
0;66	F8
0;67	F9
0;68	F10

To use Alt keys, hold down Alt as you press another key. Any key or letter may be made an Alt letter, such as Alt+P, as shown in the following table.

Keyboard Code	Alt+key
0;120 through 0;131	1, 2, 3, 4, 5, 6, 7, 8, 9, -, =
0;16 through 0;25	Q, W, E, R, T, Y, U, I, O, P
0;30 through 0;38	A, S, D, F, G, H, J, K, L
0;44 through 0;50	Z, X, C, V, B, N, M
0;104 through 0;113	F1 through F10

To use Ctrl, hold down Ctrl as you press another key, as shown in the table below.

Keyboard Code	Ctrl+key
1 through 26	A through Z
48 through 57	0 through 9
0;94 through 0;103	F1 through F10

Notice that A through Z and 0 through 9 don't have a 0; in front of them. Therefore, Ctrl+A would be

```
(prompt "\e[1;'arc';13p")
```

When you leave AutoCAD, it may be necessary to reprogram function keys to where they were originally. To reset a function key, reassign it to itself. For example, to reset F5,

```
(prompt "\e[0;63;0;63p")
```

One final cautionary note about dealing with function keys: generally, it isn't a good idea to reprogram F1 and F2. AutoCAD for Windows uses F1 for help and F2 to flip the screen back and forth between the text screen and the graphics screen.

Making One Menu Call Another

Making one menu system activate another is extremely easy. You've already learned that from a screen menu you can activate another screen menu by $S=X $S=mymenu. This line can be placed not only on the screen

menu but also on a pull-down or tablet menu. Regardless of where it's placed, it will activate the appropriate menu. $P3=mymenu $P3=* will pull down the submenu area into Pull-Down 3. It can be placed anywhere.

How to Activate a Menu From AutoLISP

Menus can also be activated from AutoLISP, as illustrated in the following example. See how the DRAW command screen menu is activated: notice that the S doesn't have a $ before it when it's used in AutoLISP.

Type: `(menucmd "S=DR") <Enter>`

This would normally be placed in an AutoLISP program. It isn't very efficient to type it in from the keyboard.

Accelerator Keys

Accelerator keys are very easy to create. In AutoCAD for Windows, any key can be reprogrammed in Release 13 to be an accelerator key. In Windows, this method is the only way you can program function keys without additional software.

A key is reprogrammed to be an accelerator key through the main base menu in effect. Reprogramming can't be done through a loadable menu. Therefore you should edit ACAD.MNU. Search for ***ACCELERATORS. You will see the following.

```
***ACCELERATORS
[CONTROL"L"]^O
[CONTROL"R"]^V
ID_Undo    [CONTROL+"Z"]
ID_Cut     [CONTROL+"X"]
ID_Copy    [CONTROL+"C"]
ID_Paste   [CONTROL+"V"]
ID_Open    [CONTROL+"O"]
ID_Print   [CONTROL+"P"]
ID_New     [CONTROL+"N"]
ID_Save    [CONTROL+"S"]
```

Here is an example of what you can add to the ***ACCELERATORS section. In brackets, enter the name of the key you want to use as your accelerator key. The name of this key must be in quotes unless it is a valid key modifier. If it is a valid key modifier, the modifier is not in quotes and is connected to the key with the + sign. For example, Ctrl+R is [CONTROL+"R"].

Following the brackets you place what you want the key to do. In the following examples, Object Snaps are used in the F3, F4 and Shift+N, and an AutoCAD command is used for Control+D.

```
["F3"]endp,int
["F4"]mid,cen
[SHIFT+"N"]nearest
[CONTROL+"D"]^c^cddinsert
```

The following are valid accelerator key modifiers:

- CONTROL
- SHIFT
- META (found on UNIX keyboards)

The function keys are enclosed in quotes, such as "F5" or "F12". Other special keys in quotes are as follows:

- "HOME"
- "END"
- "INSERT"
- "DELETE"

Moving On

As you've probably figured out by now, customizing AutoCAD requires thought, planning and work. But it's not beyond the capabilities of any user with the proper instructions. You now know how, but don't try to do it all at once. Take it one step at a time. Begin with your blocks; work them into your menu system. This is where a lot of efficiency can be achieved. And the productivity you'll realize is well worth the time it takes.

You've learned how customizable menus are. Next, you'll see that you also have the ability to create your own linetypes and hatch patterns, in addition to the linetypes and hatch patterns that AutoCAD gives you. It's easy to do, and Chapter 12 shows you how.

12

Customizing Linetypes & Hatch Patterns

Customizing Linetypes & Hatch Patterns

AutoCAD permits a lot of customization in several areas. In addition to menu systems, you can also tailor AutoCAD's linetypes and hatch patterns to your specific needs.

Although they may not seem to be related, linetypes and hatch patterns have a lot in common—at least in the way they're constructed. One of the main differences is that AutoCAD gives you a lot of help in constructing your own simple linetypes but very little in constructing your own hatch patterns.

Linetypes

Let's start with the easier one first. AutoCAD provides a function that guides you through every step (except one) to create your linetypes. Let's take it one step at a time.

A simple linetype is nothing more than lines, spaces and sometimes dots in various patterns and lengths, and AutoCAD has a unique way of describing them. Imagine a pen plotter moving in a continuous straight line. As long as the pen point is in contact with the paper, it draws a line. When the pen lifts up off the paper, nothing is drawn. Therefore, a linetype can be translated in terms of the amount of time the pen is on or off the paper. By making these times relative to each other, a linetype pattern is created.

AutoCAD uses a series of positive and negative numbers that inform the plotter how long to keep the pen lowered or raised. Positive numbers lower the pen, and negative numbers raise it. For perspective, think of .5 as the normal length of a dash and 0 as representing a dot (the pen touching the paper and immediately lifting up). Let's look at an example.

0,-.25 will produce a series of dots. In a linetype definition, the definition continues to repeat itself for as long as the line is drawn. The 0 produces the dot, and the pen is immediately lifted. The -.25 keeps the pen raised for a quarter of a time unit. Then the pattern is repeated. (A time unit is the arbitrary amount of time the pen is either lowered or raised. LTScale multiplies this time unit by the LTScale factor.)

This is how you produce a dash dot: .5,-.25,0,-.25. Notice that each time unit is separated from the next by a comma. The first .5 produces the first dash. Then the pen is lifted for a quarter of a time unit. The dot is produced by the 0, then the pen is lifted for another quarter of a time unit. The pattern repeats.

More examples of AutoCAD's standard linetypes are found in a file called ACAD.LIN. The following is a partial listing of the ACAD.LIN file that comes with Release 13.

```
;;
;;   Ver. 1.1 - AutoCAD Linetype file
;;
;;   2 variations of the linetypes have been added
;;   to this file.  One is 1/2 the original
;;   linetype and the other is double the original
;;   linetype.
;;
;;   1/28/90 - Amy Berger
;;
*BORDER,__ __ . __ __ . __ __ . __ __ . __ __ . __ __ . __ __
A,.5,-.25,.5,-.25,0,-.25
*BORDER2,__.__.__.__.__.__.__.__.__.__.__.__.__.__.__.__.__._
A,.25,-.125,.25,-.125,0,-.125
*BORDERX2,____ ____ . ____ ____ . ____ ____ . ____ ____ .
A,1.0,-.5,1.0,-.5,0,-.5

*CENTER,____ _ ____ _ ____ _ ____ _ ____ _ ____ _ ____ _ ____ _
A,1.25,-.25,.25,-.25
*CENTER2,____ _ ____ _ ____ _ ____ _ ____ _ ____ _ ____ _ ____
A,.75,-.125,.125,-.125
*CENTERX2,_____ __ _____ __ _____ __ _____ __ ____
A,2.5,-.5,.5,-.5

*DASHDOT,__ . __ . __ . __ . __ . __ . __ . __ . __ . __ . __ . _
A,.5,-.25,0,-.25
*DASHDOT2,_._._._._._._._._._._._._._._._._._._._._._._._._.
A,.25,-.125,0,-.125
*DASHDOTX2,____ . ____ . ____ . ____ . ____ . ____ . ____
A,1.0,-.5,0,-.5

*DASHED,__ __ __ __ __ __ __ __ __ __ __ __ __ __ __ __ __
A,.5,-.25
```

Creating a Linetype File

Now let's take a look at the mechanics of creating the linetypes and adding them to the linetype file. You can put your creations in any file you choose. AutoCAD uses a file called ACAD.LIN by default. Any linetype file must have the extension .LIN, which is a simple ASCII text file. Just as you would add your menus to the ACAD.MNU file, you can use your text editor to modify the file and add your own linetype. However, this isn't required, since AutoCAD has a linetype creation command that will walk you through it.

Start with a new linetype of your own creation. Your new linetype will look like this:

— — · · · — — · · · — — · · · — — · · ·

The code for this linetype is as follows:

```
.5,-.25,.5,-.25,0,-.25,0,-.25,0,-.25
```

Call your new linetype LINEDOTS.

Type: `LINETYPE <Enter>`

Response: `?/Create/Load/Set:`

Type: `Create <Enter>`

Response: `Name of linetype to create:`

Type: `LINEDOTS <Enter>`

Response: (A file dialog box asks you to pick the linetype file. It defaults to ACAD unless you have changed it.)

Type: `<Enter>` (Accept the default—your new linetype will be added to the ACAD.LIN file automatically.)

Response: `Wait, checking if linetype already defined . . .`
`Descriptive text:`

At this point, you describe what the linetype looks like. It will appear whenever you use ? with the linetype or in the linetype dialog box when you pick linetypes. You might identify it as Dash Dash Dot Dot Dot, or anything else that's meaningful to you. You also have an option here to draw a picture of the linetype. This would be a better option:

Type: `__ __ . . . __ __ . . . __ __ . . . <Enter>`

Response: `Enter pattern (on next line):`
`A,`

The cursor is now located after the A,. This is where you begin typing the pattern or numeric description of the linetype. Immediately after the A,

Type: `.5,-.25,.5,-.25,0,-.25,0,-.25,0,-.25 <Enter>`

Response: `New definition written to file.`
`?/Create/Load/Set:`

Type: `<Enter>`

This ends the linetype creation routine. The linetype is now appended to the ACAD.LIN file. Since it's a part of the ACAD.LIN file, you can use this linetype as you would any AutoCAD linetypes. It will even come up in the dialog box if the linetype file is loaded.

If you were to examine the end of the ACAD.LIN file, it should look like this:

`*LINEDOTS, __ __ . . . __ __ . . . __ __ . . .`
`A,.5,-.25,.5,-.25,0,-.25,0,-.25,0,-.25`

If you're adding to the ACAD.LIN file manually, the first line must begin with an asterisk, followed by the name of the linetype, followed by a comma, followed by the description. The second line must begin with A, then the numeric description of the linetype must follow.

What would happen if you wanted to change the definition of an existing linetype without creating a new one? This is simple. Begin as above by creating a new linetype, but give it the name of an existing linetype. AutoCAD will ask if you want to overwrite it. Answer **Y**. Then continue with the new description and definition the same way you'd create a new linetype.

If you want to delete a linetype you've created, you must go outside of AutoCAD to do it; there's no way to accomplish this from inside Auto-CAD. Remember that the linetype is stored in the ACAD.LIN file (or whatever file you created). Since these are ASCII text files, you can use your text editor to edit them. There are two lines for every file. The first line begins with an * and the second line begins with an A. When you delete these two lines, the linetype is gone.

Complex Linetypes

By editing the ACAD.LIN file you can create much more complex line-types than you're able to define using the LINETYPE command. Linetypes added directly to the ACAD.LIN file can contain not only dots and dashes of various lengths, but shapes and even text strings as well. You cannot create such complex linetypes in AutoCAD versions prior to Release 13.

The following example shows how to create a linetype containing a text string. First open the ACAD.LIN file in your text editor. Move to the very end of the file and add the following linetype definition:

```
*Boundary, Boundary Line
A,2,-.25,["BOUNDARY",Bold,S=.25,A=0,X=0.05,Y=-0.1],-1.5,1.5
```

This looks similar to the LINEDOTS definition you added to the ACAD.LIN file using the LINETYPE command. Like all linetype defini-tions, the first line must begin with an asterisk, followed by the name of the linetype (Boundary, in our example) and a verbal description (Bound-ary Line). Just as in the LINEDOTS example, the second line begins with an A, followed by the numeric description of the linetype. What is differ-ent about this complex linetype is that it contains a text string definition, enclosed within the square brackets. The generic form of a text string definition is as follows:

```
["String", Text Style, Scale, Rotation, Xoffset, Yoffset]
```

"String" is the actual text you want placed within the line. All text is enclosed within quotation marks. The Text Style is the name of the text font. If you don't include it, it uses the current style. Scale is a number whose value is the height of the text. The Rotation value has two options,

A (absolute) and R (relative), to refer to the origin of the string. The Rotation value is given in (d) degrees—the default—(r) radians or (g) gradians. Xoffset and Yoffset describe the XY axis distance the text is to be moved from the end of the last line segment, with 0 (zero) signifying no offset.

In our example, the complex linetype named Boundary draws a dashed line interspersed with the word BOUNDARY. The linetype uses Bold as the text style. It's scaled at factor .25, and offset in the XY axis from other elements.

In addition to text strings, you can also include shapes in a linetype. Like the text string definition, the shape definition is enclosed in square brackets in the second line of the linetype definition. The generic form of a shape definition is as follows:

```
[Shape Name, Shape File, Scale, Rotation, Xoffset, Yoffset]
```

Shape Name is the name of a created shape, and Shape File is the name of a compiled .SHX shape file, which contains the actual shape you want to include in your linetype. The other elements of the shape description are the same as in a text string definition.

There are a number of other linetype modifiers that you can use in complex linetype definitions:

- Linetype Scale is a scaling variable. A positive value affects both the spacing and scale of the shape you create. A negative value affects the spacing of the line but not the shape you create.
- Linetype Elaboration Offset is a shape offset value. It affects the XY axes of the shape's offset position in the linetype pattern. A negative or positive value moves the shape in the XY axes. The default offset is 0 (zero).
- Linetype Text Scale is a text modifier. It allows you to size text within the linetype. It does not affect the linetype scale.
- Linetype Rotation is a text angle modifier. It allows you to rotate the angle of the text or shape within the linetype pattern.

Hatch Patterns

Now you can use what you learned in creating a linetype to create a hatch pattern. Creating your own hatch patterns isn't the easiest thing in the world, but anyone can do it once the concepts are clear.

Just as linetypes are generally stored in the ACAD.LIN file, hatch patterns are stored in the ACAD.PAT file. All available AutoCAD hatch patterns are stored in this file as it comes to you with your AutoCAD package. Like the ACAD.LIN file, it's also an ASCII text file. It should be in the \ACADR13\COMMON\SUPPORT directory.

Here are the rules: the first line of the text file begins with an asterisk (as when you're creating a linetype). This is followed immediately by the name of the hatch pattern. The name you give it here is the name you'll eventually call it up by. The name is followed by a comma, then a brief description of the hatch pattern. Unlike a simple linetype description, it's not practical to completely describe the hatch pattern in terms of lines and dots. Therefore, this should be a verbal description of what the hatch pattern is. This description is optional, but if you include it, it will be printed when you answer **?** to the HATCH command. All available hatch patterns and their descriptions are printed out.

A Simple Hatch Pattern

To illustrate how to create a simple hatch pattern, use the LINEDOTS linetype as the model. In fact, call the hatch pattern you're creating LINEDOTS. Therefore, the first line of the hatch pattern would be

```
*linedots,Series of lines and dots
```

LINEDOTS is the name of the new hatch pattern, and the name is followed by a description of the pattern.

The lines that follow this first line numerically describe the hatch pattern; each line describes a single pass over the hatch pattern. Have you ever watched AutoCAD draw a hatch pattern? It doesn't draw the entire pattern all at once. Watch the Brick hatch pattern as an example. It first goes over the entire pattern with horizontal lines. When that part of the pattern is complete, it begins again with vertical lines. If you watch the Honey pattern, you'll see several passes before the pattern is complete. Imagine that each pass is the same as a linetype. And if you can produce enough linetypes in exactly the right order and line them up, you can produce a hatch pattern. (In our example we'll use a single pass, to keep it simple.)

Each pass represents a single line following the hatch pattern name and description. This is called a line family. There are four parts to every line in the line family:

- Angle
- X,Y Origin
- Offset-X, Offset-Y
- Penlift pattern

Look at the following example:

```
*LINEDOTS,Series of lines and dots
0, 0,0, 0,.5, .5,-.25,0,-.25,0,-.25
```

This pattern draws a series of dashes and two dots at a 0-degree angle with a .5-unit separation between each line unit. (See Figure 12-1.)

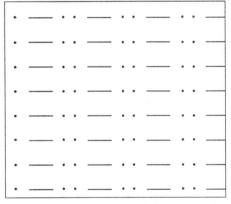

Figure 12-1: The LINEDOTS custom hatch pattern.

The following table breaks down the four parts of the single line in the LINEDOTS hatch pattern.

Pattern Part	LINEDOTS Value
Angle	0,
X,Y Origin	0,0,
Offset-X, Offset-Y	0,.5,
Penlift pattern	.5,-.25,0,-.25,0,-.25

Each part of the line definition ends with a comma, and the parts are separated by one or more spaces.

The first 0, determines the "Angle" at which the line is to be drawn. Since it's a 0, the first line in the pass is drawn horizontally. Be careful not to confuse the angle you put here with the rotation question used with the HATCH command. Think of a hatch pattern as a successive series of lines drawn from left to right, then down to up.

The next group establishes the "Origin" of the hatch pattern. This has nothing to do with your drawing's absolute origin. The absolute origin of all hatch patterns is 0,0 regardless of where in the drawing the hatch begins. What you're entering here is the point of origin for this pass, relative to the absolute point of origin. Remember, the first pass is from 0,0—the origin of the hatch pattern. (See the "A Two-Pass Hatch Pattern" section below for more about working with origins.)

Understanding the origin of the various passes is relatively easy. The "Offset-X" and "Offset-Y" are not so easy. (In the AutoCAD guides these are called delta-x and delta-y. "Offset" seems a little more descriptive to most people.) The offset is the origin of each line as it's drawn, relative to the line drawn before. Look at Figure 12-2. This is a 45-degree line drawn with a 0 offset.

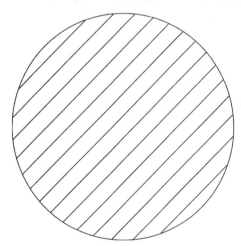

Figure 12-2: Forty-five degree lines drawn with no offset.

This means that the line pattern on the second line up is drawn exactly the same as the line pattern below. As you can see, this gives the effect of nothing but a series of slanted lines. Look at what happens in Figure 12-3 when the lines, as they go up, are offset .5 in the X direction and .5 in the Y direction. This is the purpose of Offset-X and Offset-Y.

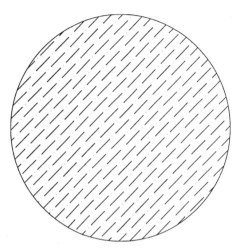

Figure 12-3: The same lines drawn with X and Y offsets.

Remember that the hatch pattern will begin at an arbitrary origin, and proceed to draw a group from left to right, then advance upward in the Y direction. .5,.5 means that each successive line in the pattern will move to the right .5 units and up .5 units. This results in the .5 spacing over and up between the lines. The offset is always relative to the initial angle given in the line, so that angle forms the X axis for the offset.

It's clear enough that you offset the Y value to give you spacing between the lines. Why, though, would you want to offset the X value, and what effect does it have? You can see the results in Figure 12-3. But also imagine a brick wall. Each successive line of bricks is offset to the right a little, to create a pattern. So .5,1 would space the bricks upward by one unit and every other line would offset .5 to the right of the origin, creating a staircase effect.

The final group in the LINEDOTS hatch definition is the dash, dash, dot, dot, dot pattern, the same pattern used for creating linetypes. Remember, all positive numbers represent the number of unit spacings with the pen held down. A 0 represents a dot. The negative numbers represent the number of unit spacings with the pen lifted up. When creating the pattern, you're limited to a total of six pen definitions (i.e., the pen can only go up or down a total of six times). Notice that the pattern we're using in Figure 12-1 is similar to the linetype created earlier in this chapter, though it can't be exactly like the linetype pattern because of this pen-definition limitation.

A Two-Pass Hatch Pattern

Now, what effect would a second line in a line family have? Let's see if we can create a hatch pattern with a series of Xs, which will also illustrate how both the origin and the offset affect the pattern. We'll define a first pass that will draw lines angled at 45 degrees. Once all those lines are drawn, the next pass will draw another set of lines at 135 degrees through the first set, thus forming a series of Xs.

Start with the first pattern:

```
*XS,Series of Xs
45, 0,0, .5,.5, .5,-.5
135, 0,0, .5,.5, .5,-.5
```

The first pass will angle at 45 degrees (producing one half of the Xs). The origin is at 0,0. Offset-X and Offset-Y are .5,.5. The pattern is .5,-.5. This draws a line at a 45-degree angle for .5 units, then picks up the pen for .5 time unit, then continues with the next line as it goes across. The next line begins with the offset .5,.5 and continues.

After the first pass is completed, the next pass draws a line at a 135-degree angle (the second half of the Xs). Notice that the origin is the same as for the first pass. The offset is the same as the first pass with the same pattern. Since the origin for both passes is at 0,0, you get a pattern that looks like Figure 12-4. Notice that the legs of the Xs connect. As you can see, they don't look like Xs. It's an interesting pattern, but it's not what you were trying to create.

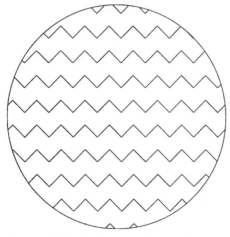

Figure 12-4: Both passes have the same origin (not the effect we want).

To correct this, the origin of the second pass must begin to the right of the origin of the first pass, so that the foot of the base of the 45-degree angle line starts at 0,0 and the foot of the base of the 135-degree angle line starts at .375,0.

```
*XS,Series of Xs
45, 0,0, .5,.5, .5,-.5
135, .375,0, .5,.5, .5,-.5
```

The origin of the second pass was changed to .375,0. This causes the base of the second line of the X .375 to start to the right of the first and gives us what we want. (See Figure 12-5.)

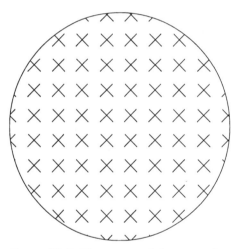

Figure 12-5: The origin of the second pass has now been moved to the right.

Editing ACAD.PAT

Now that you've created a hatch pattern, what do you do with it? Remember that it goes into a file called ACAD.PAT. Unfortunately, there's no convenient AutoCAD command for creating hatch patterns, as there is for linetypes. Therefore, you must do it all yourself. Try one. Create the XS hatch pattern above. Use your text editor and edit ACAD.PAT. This file is probably in the \ACADR13\COMMON\SUPPORT directory. Add the following lines at the end of the file.

Type: EDIT <Enter>

Response: File to edit:

Type: ACAD.PAT <Enter>

This file is not extremely large, so it should all fit into memory, unlike the ACAD.MNU file. Go to the very end of the ACAD.PAT file an add the following three lines of code:

```
*XS,Series of Xs
45, 0,0, .5,.5, .5,-.5
135, .375,0, .5,.5, .5,-.5
```

Save the ACAD.PAT file and exit the text editor.

Now the hatch pattern can be used almost like any other hatch pattern. Let's give it a try. Draw a circle. Use the BHATCH command and pick the drop list box and go to the bottom of the list. Behold, your pattern should be there. You will not see the pattern in the preview box, but it will be in the list box. Now let's use the hatch pattern. Hatch the circle. The hatch pattern should look like Figure 12-5.

Have you ever wondered why some hatch pattern scales are different than others? This is because of the line pattern used. If you use a 1,-.5,0,-.5, the 1 will draw a larger line than the .25. Therefore, hatch lines will be larger and consequently need a smaller scale. So, when you're creating your own hatch patterns, try to keep them relatively the same size as other hatch patterns. (This is a very big order when you consider that Auto-CAD's own hatch patterns are not consistent.)

Moving On

Making your own hatch patterns is not difficult and can add a degree of personalization to your system. Although AutoCAD supplies a large number of hatch patterns, third-party companies have made a lot of money selling hatch patterns, since it's often necessary to purchase a number of these sets to get everything you want. Don't be afraid to spend a little time and create a pattern if you need one. The development of your own hatch patterns may not be your most pressing requirement, but it's one more link in the total customization chain that will help you develop a CAD system that serves your company's needs.

13

Out-of-the-Box Productivity Tips

Out-of-the-Box Productivity Tips

So far, we've concentrated on how you can address your specific needs and increase your productivity by changing the AutoCAD program and finding new ways to interface with it. Now let's change the emphasis to things you can do to increase your productivity with AutoCAD just as it comes from the box.

An interesting thing about AutoCAD is that there's no *one* way to do a task. You can often find as many as five ways to accomplish the same thing. Some users may interpret this to mean AutoCAD is too complicated compared to other CAD systems. But this is unfair. AutoCAD is a very rich CAD system that gives its users a variety of ways to accomplish a wide range of tasks. According to individual taste, each user can decide on the best way to accomplish those tasks, given the options at hand. Without all these options, AutoCAD's capabilities would be so limited that many of the program features we take for granted wouldn't be available. In fact, many of us would welcome even more program features.

Even though you're not limited to one way of doing a task, certain methods will be more productive than others. A prime example of this is illustrated in Figure 13-1. Here you see two lines. A circle has been drawn tangent to each of these lines with a given radius, using the TTR CIRCLE command.

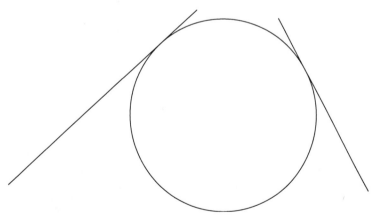

Figure 13-1: Begin with Circle TTR.

In Figure 13-2, we've broken each line at the point of tangency to the end of the line.

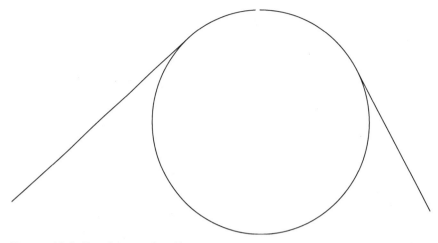

Figure 13-2: Break to ends of lines.

In Figure 13-3, we've broken the circle counterclockwise from the point of tangency of one line to the point of tangency of another line. We're left with a fillet between the two lines with a fixed radius.

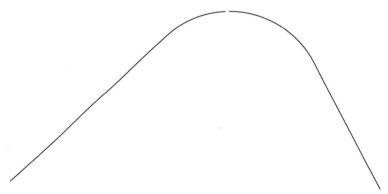

Figure 13-3: Break greater arc of circle.

This is one way to accomplish the task, but you probably realize that this is the long way; instead, you could just use the FILLET command.

This is an example of a method that makes you less productive than you could be. No one would deny that this method works—but there's a better way. In this chapter you're going to learn that what you're doing isn't necessarily wrong; it just may not be the most efficient way to get the job done.

Prototype Drawings

As you know, many parameters must be in place in order to properly set up a drawing. If you had to set up everything from scratch for each new drawing, you might never have the heart to start. Just look at a few of the program features that you can set:

- Attributes
- Units
- Limits
- Linetypes
- Text styles
- Dimension variables
- Dimension styles
- Layers
- Blocks
- Title blocks
- Snap, Grid, Ortho, views, beginning zoom level
- Viewport configurations
- Saved views
- View point coordination
- LTSCALE
- Fonts
- Plotting parameters
- Color
- System variables
- Saved User Coordinate System(s)

And that's not all; parameters may change from one drawing to the next. In fact, you can probably come up with as many as three, four or more standard drawing setups, depending on your drawing needs and the degree of your discipline. Then how can all of these drawing needs be satisfied with standard prototypes when you begin a new drawing?

ACAD.DWG

When AutoCAD is installed out of the box, one of the AutoCAD directory files is ACAD.DWG, AutoCAD's standard prototype drawing, which is what you use when you begin a new drawing. Therefore, the easiest way to establish your own prototype is to edit ACAD.DWG, which you do by first changing to the directory that contains your main AutoCAD programs. Let's assume that this directory is C:\ACADR13\COMMON\SUPPORT. If your particular directory or hard drive is different, substitute your drive and directory.

Now open up the ACAD.DWG file. It should be located in the \ACADR13\COMMON\SUPPORT directory. Once the drawing is visible, make changes to it in accordance with what you want your drawing to look like at that stage. Use the outline of variables to prompt you for things that need to be set up. When the drawing is exactly as you want it, save the drawing. Remember to set your zoom level to where you want it when the new drawing starts. The ACAD.DWG file is then saved to your AutoCAD support directory.

Next, begin AutoCAD the way you normally do. When you start a new drawing, it will look exactly like the ACAD.DWG file you just modified.

There's nothing magical about ACAD.DWG—it's just another drawing. You can make your default prototype drawing anything you choose. Note that this is your *default* prototype drawing. You can have an unlimited number of prototype drawings, but only one default prototype. And when AutoCAD is first installed out of the box, the name of that default prototype drawing is ACAD.

You can change the name, and the directory, of the default prototype drawing. When you configure AutoCAD, Item 7 is Configure Operating Parameters. Item 2, Initial Drawing Setup, is a submenu to Item 7.

Response: `Enter name of default prototype file for new drawings or . for none <ACAD>:`

In this initial setup, AutoCAD defaults to ACAD.DWG. At this point, you can change the prototype drawing's name and directory by typing in the name of another drawing. If you change the name, be certain you're changing it to a drawing that exists. If the drawing you change it to doesn't exist, AutoCAD will give you an error message the next time you begin a new drawing—unless you tell AutoCAD to start the new drawing without a prototype.

Beginning a New Drawing

There is an easy way to create and easily access a whole library of proto-type drawings. One of the things about a library is that most of the items should be in the same place. In versions of AutoCAD before Release 12, this didn't seem to matter for prototype drawings. When you used the command NEWDWG=PROTODWG, AutoCAD wasn't able to find PROTODWG unless it was your default prototype or you gave it the drive path specifications. This is no longer the case.

You can have a whole library of prototype drawings and keep them in a single directory. Let's say you call it C:\PROTO. Place all of your proto-type drawings in this directory. Next, tell AutoCAD not only where to find your prototype drawings but which one is to be your default proto-type drawing. To do this, begin a new drawing. You are given a Create New Drawing dialog box. Pick Prototype. This brings up a Prototype Drawing File dialog box. Click in the directories list box and select the C:\PROTO directory. This changes the default directory to C:\PROTO. Now pick in the File Name list box the drawing you want to be your prototype, and pick OK. This returns you to the Create New Drawing dialog box. Now pick the Retain as Default check box. You can give the new drawing a name or not. What matters this first time is that you OK the dialog box.

You've just created a default prototype drawing. This could be ACAD.DWG or any other drawing you might want to make the default prototype. It's important here that, in carrying out this process, you also told AutoCAD where to find *all* your prototype drawings—as long as the default prototype drawing is in the same directory as the rest. From now on you can choose any prototype drawing by just picking Prototype and picking the drawing. The default directory will contain your prototype drawing library.

Remember that any drawing can be made the default by picking the Retain as Default check box before you OK the new drawing.

One situation that might call for beginning a new drawing without a prototype is when you need to import a DXF or IGES file. DXF requires that you begin with a new drawing; if the drawing is not new, DXFIN will import objects only. DXFIN is the command used to import a DXF file. Many users go around in circles beginning what they think is a new drawing, only to have AutoCAD tell them it is not a new drawing and that only objects will be imported. The problem is that you're almost always beginning a new drawing with a prototype, so your "new" drawing is actually a copy of an existing drawing. This occurs every time you're using DXFIN. Just remember to check the No Prototype check box on the Create New Drawing dialog box to get around the problem of having only your objects imported into the drawing.

Object Snaps

One of the major obstacles to AutoCAD productivity is the improper use of Object Snaps. Object Snaps are valuable and should be used at all times, but access to them is awkward. There are several ways to efficiently get at Object Snaps. Release 13 gives you *cursor menus*; use them.

One of the best ways to get at Object Snaps is to reprogram your function keys. (See Chapter 11, "Using Multiple Menu Systems," for details on how to do this.) Another option is to reprogram your mouse buttons to make one or more of them Object Snaps.

Even if you have just a two- or three-button mouse you can still program at least one of your buttons with the Object Snaps you use the most. Let's assume you have a three-button mouse: the first button is Pick; the second button is Enter (which should be left as it is, since it's used to cancel most commands, confirm selection sets and repeat the last command); the third button is preset to your cursor menu. Remember, you now have menu program options of Buttons 2 and 3 as Ctrl and Ctrl+Shift respectively.

The question now is, which Object Snap should you choose? Fortunately, Object Snaps can be combined. Endpoint and Intersection are the two that most people use 80 percent of the time. Why not combine them?

On one of the button menus, place the following line:

```
int,endp
```

It would be extremely rare for AutoCAD to make a mistake and use the wrong one. Combining these two Object Snaps not only works but actually saves you time. Have you ever used Object Snap Intersection only to receive the error message that no intersection was found? Then you had to change it to Endpoint. This will eliminate that problem and save a button as well.

Using Attributes for Fast Text

Almost everyone who uses AutoCAD has occasion to create and fill out a table of information. Most AutoCAD users still choose the TEXT or DTEXT command to do this. And MTEXT is not a good option for tables. But no text command is really the most efficient way to accomplish this task.

One of the best uses for ATTRIBUTES has nothing to do with extracting data from an AutoCAD drawing; it's an ideal way of entering large amounts of text, especially text in chart form. The following is a step-by-step method for using ATTRIBUTES to make a text chart.

Begin by making a blank chart like the one in Figure 13-4. The following is only an example. Once the chart is made, you're ready to begin building your attributes.

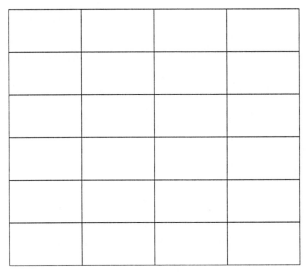

Figure 13-4: Beginning table grid.

Choose Attribute from the Construct pull-down menu, or from the keyboard enter the ATTDEF command as follows:

Type: attdef <Enter>

Response: Attribute modes—Invisible:N Constant:N Verify:N Preset:N
Enter (ICVP) to change; <RETURN> when done:

Press: <Enter> (Make sure Invisible is N.)

Response: `Attribute tag:`

Type: `Part <Enter>`

Response: `Attribute prompt:`

Press: `<Enter>` (You may put in a different prompt if you want to. If you leave it blank, the prompt will be the attribute tag.)

Response: `Default attribute value:`

Press: `<Enter>` (You may enter a default attribute value.)

Response: `Start point or Align/Center/Fit/Middle/Right/Style`

Now pick a point in the first block where you want the Part to be. (*Hint:* Make the point relative to the intersection of the block. This is where your text will start.)

The following are typical prompts:

Response: `Height:`

Type: (Enter an appropriate height for the text.)

Response: `Rotation angle:`

Type: (Enter an appropriate rotation for the text. Typically, this is 0.)

At this point, the word Part will be written in the first block. Repeat the above ATTDEF command for each of the items in the chart—Number, Vendor and Room. Your chart will look like Figure 13-5.

PART	NUMBER	VENDOR	ROOM

Figure 13-5: Table attributes.

You're now ready for the next step: blocking the attributes.

Type: `Block <Enter>`

Response: `Block name:`

Type: `TABLE <Enter>`

Response: `Insertion base point`

Type: (Pick the intersection where Part begins.)

Response: `Select objects:`

Now pick each attribute in the order you want to be prompted for a value. Then press Enter to confirm the selection. If you did it correctly, all the attributes will disappear.

Notice in this example that no object was actually blocked. The attributes themselves are the only things that make up the block called TABLE.

Now you're ready to fill out your chart using the INSERT command. Choose Insert from the Draw pull-down menu, or from the keyboard enter the INSERT command as follows:

Type: `Insert <Enter>`

Response: `Block name:`

Type:	`TABLE <Enter>`	
Response:	`Insertion base point:`	
Type:	(Pick the intersection of the square where you want the Part to begin.)	
Response:	`X Scale factor`	
Press:	`<Enter>`	
Response:	`Y Scale factor`	
Press:	`<Enter>` (Notice these are the regular INSERT questions.)	
Response:	`Rotation angle:`	
Press:	`<Enter>`	

Response:	`Enter attribute values`
	`Part:`
	`Number:`
	`Vendor:`
	`Room:`	

The above questions are asked one at a time. Enter the appropriate response. When all questions are asked, the text will be placed in the appropriate square. (See Figure 13-6.)

PART	NUMBER	VENDOR	ROOM
K305	33	Ace	305
B406	20	Braker	201
C701	50	Chadka	200

Figure 13-6: Insert block.

If the system variable ATTDIA is set to 1 when you insert the block, you can answer the questions through the Enter Attributes dialog box. (See Figure 13-7.)

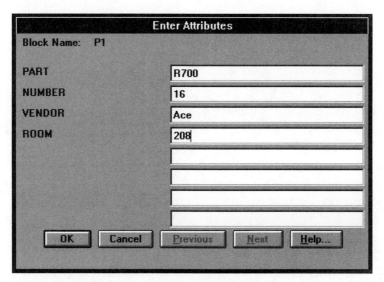

Figure 13-7: The Enter Attributes dialog box.

Editing the text is a snap. Enter the DDATTE command and use the dialog box for editing as well. Just point to the line of text and change the items in the dialog box.

This technique is not limited to charts and tables. It can be used effectively anywhere you need to place text that has some geometric reference point. This is an ideal system for filling out title blocks, parts lists or bills of materials, for example. Use your own imagination.

Good Backup Procedure

Nothing is less productive than repeating something that you've already done. But that's exactly what can happen if you lose your only copy of your latest work. Very few companies have anything that comes close to a fail-safe backup procedure. Of course, it could be argued that there's no such thing as a foolproof system. But you should make it a top priority to be as prepared as possible for an emergency.

Ask yourself this question: What would you do if you came to work tomorrow, turned on the computer and discovered that all your files were lost? This is a real possibility, and the only smart way to deal with it is to be prepared. You must have a contingency plan—a backup.

How you back up your computer(s) usually depends on the hardware available to you. If you have a tape backup system, it's simple. Label your tapes with a different tape for Monday, Tuesday, Wednesday, etc. Then use that day's tape, and back up the entire hard disk. With the proper tape backup system, this shouldn't be a huge chore as long as you do it regularly. This gives you enough generations for most eventualities. But, as you'll see, even this isn't always enough.

The problem comes when you're backing up onto floppies. Because this method is so time-consuming, it's easy to put off doing it. That's when you leave yourself open to disaster.

Unless you have a small hard disk, it's not practical to back up the entire hard disk to floppies every day. So you need to do some selective organization. Certain portions of your hard disk don't need to be backed up: the AutoCAD programs, the DOS directory, or any other program whose original disk is in safekeeping in another location. A special disk containing a one-time copy of your root directory should be available, as well as another disk with a one-time copy of any software necessary to restore backup disks (if you're using backup software that's not part of DOS). And if you're backing up with a tape drive, you should have a disk ready to go with the root directory and the software that runs the tape drive.

Only *data* needs to be backed up on a regular basis. Assuming that your only data files worth worrying about are your AutoCAD drawings, what's the proper procedure for keeping them safe with the least amount of effort, using floppies only? That depends on your file organization. One way is to create a directory off the root directory, called \DRAWINGS. Then place all your drawings in a subdirectory of \DRAWINGS. In most cases, by backing up the \DRAWINGS directory and its subdirectories, you can back up all your AutoCAD drawings with a single command.

If you're using DOS, this is the procedure:

Type: `CD\DRAWINGS` `<Enter>` (To be active in the \DRAWINGS directory on the proper drive.)

Response: `C:\DRAWINGS>`

The above response assumes a PG PROMPT and that your
\DRAWINGS directory is on the C: drive of a DOS machine.

Type: `BACKUP C:*.* A:*.DWG /S <Enter>`

This is the command for the DOS BACKUP.COM program supplied on
your DOS disk. Beginning with DOS 6.0, other backup schemes have been
developed. The point is that you use one. This example assumes that this
program is on your hard drive (usually in the \DOS directory) and that
you're pathed to the \DOS directory. The /S tells the backup program to
back up the \DRAWINGS directory and all of its subdirectories. This
backs up all of your drawings.

You must have enough formatted floppy disks on hand to do the job.
You'll insert these one by one as requested by the program. When the
backup is through, this group of floppies forms a dataset. They should be
labeled in the order they were inserted, as DATASET 1, Disk 1. If you
used 10 disks, they will be DATASET 1, Disks 1 through 10. If you ever
need to restore information, you'll insert the disks in that order.

Be sure to back up *at least* once a week, and even more often if you've
done a lot of work. The rule is that the frequency of backup is determined
by how much work you're willing to lose compared to how much time it
takes to back up. By backing up once a week, you're saying that, if you
lose everything on your hard disk, you're willing to be behind no more
than one week.

Now say it's week number two. Can you use the same disks you used
to back up last week? The answer is a resounding *no!* If you back up onto
the same disks, you'll be destroying your only existing backup. Therefore,
create DATASET 2.

On the third week it's okay to back up on DATASET 1. Each week,
alternate between DATASETS 1 and 2. (If something goes wrong during a
backup, *never* pick up the other backup and back up onto it.)

But this still is not enough. You need DATASET 3. Once a month, back
up on DATASET 3 in addition to, not instead of, the backup you normally
do. Then take DATASET 3 home with you. If the office or building you
work in suffers damage from a fire or natural disaster, your insurance
company may replace your computers—but who's going to replace your
data? Keep a recent backup (no older than one month) off the premises.

SAVE Frequently

A routine backup procedure should protect you from major disasters. But fortunately, major disasters are not that frequent. Minor disasters are much more likely to happen. For example, how much do you lose when AutoCAD freezes and a drawing in memory is lost?

Use the SAVE command to save your drawings at least every 30 minutes. This may seem like a lot, especially if it takes several minutes to perform the save. But it's nothing compared to several hours' or even an entire day's work.

The best way to use the SAVE command is to add suffix 1 and suffix 2 to the drawing name with each SAVE. Assume the name of the drawing is NEWDWG. After the first 30 minutes of work, save it as NEWDWG1; after the next 30 minutes, save it as NEWDWG2. Alternate every half hour just as you alternate datasets every week.

Remember also that the SAVE command destroys first the drawing to which it is being saved. When you finish for the day and end your drawing, you have three versions of the same drawing: NEWDWG, NEWDWG1 and NEWDWG2. When you're sure everything's all right, you can delete the temporary saved files. (This method also gives you a three-generation backup while you're in the drawing.) Never depend on the automatic save feature of AutoCAD. It is for emergencies only. It *doesn't* mean you don't have to save. If you do need this automatic backup file, it is probably named AUTO.SV$ if you haven't changed its name. Before you go into another drawing you must rename this file to a .DWG extension. Then you can load it as any other drawing. If you mistakenly go into another drawing then you run the risk of having this file overwritten.

Copy to a Floppy

But you're still not through. What if you go to lunch and come back to find that lightning has caused a power failure and everything on your computer is gone, including the three saved versions on your hard disk? Even if you're using a tape backup system, the latest version of your current drawing is at least one day old. What about all the work you did this morning? Here's the solution: *never* leave your machine without copying your current work to a scratch floppy. And at the end of the day, copy the entire day's work onto a floppy before going home.

Careful users generally run with a safety or scratch floppy in their computers. The moment you complete a drawing, copy it to the project floppy.

When you finish the project, make two floppy copies. Take one floppy set off-site for storage. Through it all, feel free to reuse the scratch floppy.

All of this may seem like a lot of trouble. You may think that if you do all this, you won't have time to draw—and what kind of productivity is that? Believe me when I tell you that this is the minimum you need to do for safety, and that even this is not totally fail-safe.

When you're using AutoCAD, or any electronic program, you're putting your company's future at the mercy of unpredictable magnetic blips, sunspots and other natural phenomena. But if you follow these recommendations, you're protected from total disaster.

One final word of caution: Use the DOS command RESTORE to *restore* information from time to time, because backups themselves may not restore in some circumstances—if, for example, the tape is defective, if data is corrupted, or if, for a variety of other reasons, you may think you're backing up, only to find when you try to restore that nothing is there.

Object Filters

AutoCAD has a SELECT ALL option and an Object Selection Filters dialog box. (See Figure 13-8.) The beauty of object filters is that they select all of a certain group of objects, whether they can be seen or not. In other words, none of the objects are inaccessible, because they're on layers that are Off or Frozen. Objects that match the selection criteria are selected without condition.

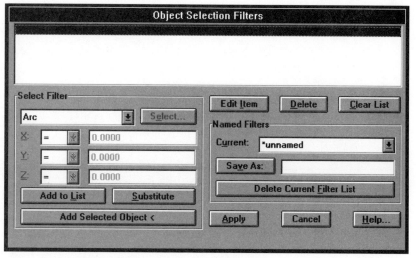

Figure 13-8: Object Selection Filters dialog box.

The (ssget "x") AutoLISP Command

The AutoLISP command for Select Objects, (ssget), is the simplest filter of all. When the "x" is added without any parameters, all objects in the database are selected. When do you use a SELECT ALL command? Any time AutoCAD asks you to select objects. Simply enter **(ssget "x")**. Of course you can also just enter **ALL**. But here we're going to show you a quick way to filter selections without using the dialog box.

All objects in the database will be selected (they're all highlighted). Then confirm with Enter to activate the AutoCAD command that asked you to select objects.

The need for this command is apparent in many instances. For example, if you want to move or rotate the objects in your drawing, you run the risk of not selecting all objects. Have you ever had this happen, because objects on Off or Frozen layers didn't get moved? Well, this command will prevent that from happening.

On the other hand, let's say you don't want to select all objects. Can you select only certain objects? Yes you can, with a variation of the command. But, first, let's explain some things about objects.

There are various *kinds* of objects, such as line, circle, arc and text. Each object has specific designations or properties: the layer it's on, its color and, if it's a block, its name. Each of these aspects is identified by a code number. The following table shows some object aspects and their codes:

Code	Object Aspect
0	Type object
2	Block
6	Linetype
7	Text style
8	Layer
38	Elevation
39	Thickness
62	Color
66	Attributes

You can use these codes to select objects according to various criteria. Suppose you wanted to select all the line objects in your drawing. When asked to select objects, enter the following:

```
(ssget "x" '((0 . "LINE"))) <Enter>
```

This tells AutoCAD to select all line objects. The 0 is for object type and LINE is in quotation marks. If you wanted to select all polylines, for example, substitute "POLYLINE" for "LINE".

If you wanted all lines on layer MECH, you'd combine the two specifications as follows:

```
(ssget "x" '((0 . "LINE")(8 . "MECH"))) <Enter>
```

(0 . "LINE") selects the object type. (8 . "MECH") chooses only those lines on layer (8) MECH. When you combine two or more, all objects and criteria must be specified.

The above rules originally applied to Releases 10 and 11, but the (ssget) command's filter capability was expanded in Release 11, then expanded further in Release 12. In the preceding example, objects can be filtered only with an "and"; therefore, it will bring in only line objects on layer MECH. However, if you're using Release 11 or Release 12, you can include an "or," as shown in the following example.

First, assume you have one line, one arc and one circle on layer MECH and only one line on layer 0.

```
(ssget "x" '((0 . "LINE") (8 . "MECH")))
```

This example will filter in only the one line found on layer MECH—not the line found on layer 0 or the circle found on layer MECH. Prior to Release 11, you couldn't secure only the line and the circle on layer MECH, because the constructs were considered to be "and" only. Therefore, you couldn't specify a line *or* a circle on layer MECH. But now look at the new construction with Release 11:

```
(ssget "x" '((0 . "LINE,CIRCLE")(8 . "MECH")))
```

Notice that LINE and CIRCLE are separated by a comma. This is the way you construct an "or" sequence. What you're saying is, give me a line *or* a circle that's on layer MECH. You can make this sequence as complicated as you want by specifying a series of "or" layers; for example, (8 . "MECH,TXT,DIM") would have asked for a line or a circle on layers MECH, TXT or DIM.

Single-Keystroke Abbreviations

One of the most productive methods of accessing commands is through keystroke abbreviations from the keyboard. It might surprise you to hear that you needn't have expert typing skills to increase your productivity through single-keystroke commands. In fact, this method may be easier if you aren't a touch typist, because it sometimes takes longer for a touch typist to seek out individual key locations.

The following will permit you to use one- or two-keystroke commands without using the ***ACCELERATOR section of the menu. After all, this generally will be used for function keys and Ctrl and Shift keys in combination with other keys.

Can you type the letter L and the spacebar with one hand faster than you can use your screen menus or pick the LINE command from the tablet? Once you're familiar with this technique, your answer will be a resounding yes. This is why a single-keystroke command is more efficient.

The term *single* keystroke is a little misleading. There are only 26 letters in the alphabet and many more than 26 AutoCAD commands, so we're really talking about single *and* double keystrokes. In this chapter, we'll try to cover all the major AutoCAD commands that can be accessed with one and two keystrokes followed by the spacebar or Enter; to simplify the discussion, though, we'll call them all single-keystroke commands.

You can always add one- or two-letter aliases in the ACAD.PGP file. I don't recommend this, however, because it is not as flexible as getting a little help from AutoLISP. AutoLISP can do the job very effectively. So let's look at how this can be done.

AutoCAD users have or can create a file called ACAD.LSP. It is generally placed in one of the SUPPORT directories. It does not come with AutoCAD, but you can create it if it doesn't exist. This special AutoLISP file is loaded every time you enter the drawing editor; therefore, it's an ideal place to put your single-keystroke commands to ensure that they're always available to you. Now let's look at the simplest way to create a single-keystroke command.

Assume you want the letter L to mean LINE. Although this is a standard alias in the ACAD.PGP file it serves as an example and AutoCAD will use the AutoLISP routine before it will use the ACAD.PGP alias. Therefore repeating it in the AutoLISP file does not harm and actually saves a little bit of memory. Type the following at the command line:

```
Type:  (defun C:L () (command "LINE")) <Enter>
```

Now let's try it.

Type: L <Enter>

Response: From point:

As you can see, you've made the letter L stand for the AutoCAD LINE command. You actually created an AutoLISP program called "L" that issues the LINE command. It's as simple as that.

The following is a recommended list of abbreviations for you to consider. You can assign any of these abbreviations using the same AutoLISP syntax that you used for the L abbreviation and the LINE command above.

Abbreviation	Command	Abbreviation	Command
A	ARC	MR	MIRRORYPE
B	BREAK	MS	MSPACE
C	CIRCLE	MZ	MEASURE
CH	DDCHPROP	O	OFFSET
CF	CHAMFER	P	PLINE
DL	DIMLINEAR	PE	PEDIT
DS	DIST	PS	PSPACE
DI	DIVIDE	Q	QSAVE
DT	DTEXT	R	ROTATE
E	ERASE	S	SNAP
EX	EXTEND	SC	SCALE
F	FILLET	ST	STRETCH
G	GRID	SV	SAVE
H	BHATCH	T	TRIM
I	DDINSERT	TX	MTEXT
K	COPY	V	'VIEW
L	LINE	W	WBLOCK
LA	DDLMODES	X	EXPLODE
LN	LINET	Z	'ZOOM

Model Space & Paper Space

AutoCAD has two operating modes—Model Space and Paper Space. Let's review the two modes as factors of productivity. Model Space is the traditional 2D or 3D geometry mode that AutoCAD has always had. Paper Space is a limited 2D geometry mode that lets you place multiple scaled drawings on the same sheet. Paper Space lets you open up and organize your viewports. It also lets you annotate the drawing, then plot out all the scaled drawing views together. In reality Paper Space lets you treat the paper as a 1:1 and compose your model drawing on it.

To avoid confusion, you need to think of Paper Space and Model Space as different ways of viewing and working with and within your drawing. Each has its own set of commands. You must use the commands that relate to the mode you're in.

The initial command that permits you to work in Paper Space is TILEMODE. This is really a system variable, but it's used as an AutoCAD command. If TILEMODE is set to 1, you can only work in Model Space; if TILEMODE is set to 0, you can work in Paper Space and Model Space. By toggling between these two modes, you can effectively maintain two presentations of a single drawing in memory at the same time—and thus enhance your productivity.

Paper Space Viewports

The primary purpose of Paper Space is to open an unlimited number of viewports, so that you can work in those viewports, arrange the viewports anywhere on the screen (paper), then plot the screen as you see it. Because you can toggle back and forth between different views, there's a tendency to think of the two modes as two different drawings. They are not. Anything done to any view or any part of an object while in Paper Space *edits* that object. Remember, you have only one set of objects. Paper Space just gives you more flexibility in viewing and plotting those objects.

In Paper Space, you can create an unlimited number of viewports, using the MVIEW command. Once you've created these viewports, you can move them around the background where they reside, or you can enter them directly to work on the model itself.

PSPACE & MSPACE Commands

Within Paper Space, besides the MVIEW command, there are two additional modes—PSPACE and MSPACE. This also causes confusion. The important thing to remember is that you're still in Paper Space mode. You toggle between these two internal modes with the PSPACE and MSPACE commands. This lets you work in Paper Space and Model Space as needed.

When you're in PSPACE, you can't enter the viewports to change anything, but you can move the viewports around on the screen and draw on the background. MSPACE lets you enter the Model Space or active viewport. Notice that the crosshairs of your digitizer or mouse are confined to the viewport border.

When you're in MSPACE, the normal UCS icons appear in each viewport. Notice that one of your viewports has a double outline: this is your active viewport. If you move your cursor inside this viewport, your crosshairs become active. If you move the cursor to any other viewport, the crosshairs turn into an arrow, indicating an inactive viewport. If you pick while you're inside another viewport, that viewport becomes active.

While you're in the MSPACE mode of Paper Space, the viewports you created will act the same as the traditional viewports in Model Space— with two notable advantages. First, you can have as many viewports as you need. Second, if you enter PSPACE mode within Paper Space, you can move the viewports around, make them larger or smaller, annotate them anywhere on the screen with text, draw from one to another and plot exactly what you see on the screen.

In addition to the MVIEW, MSPACE and PSPACE commands, another new command, VPLAYER, allows you to freeze and thaw layers, because it's viewport-specific. TILEMODE must be set to 0 for VPLAYER to operate. If you accidentally entered VPLAYER while in the MSPACE mode, AutoCAD would automatically switch you to PSPACE in order to select your viewports, then return you back to your original screen mode. Another important factor to remember is that the AutoCAD commands STRETCH, ERASE and MOVE don't work in this mode.

Productivity With Model Space & Paper Space

So how does this increase your productivity? Paper Space is designed to let you compose multiple drawing views on the same sheet, then plot them all out together. To understand the concept, think of the background of Paper Space in PSPACE mode as a sheet of poster board onto which you'll place several models and move them around until they're positioned correctly.

Imagine that you need three views of your model. By using the MVIEW command, each view can be arranged in its own viewport. Now, when you toggle back to PSPACE, the individual viewports are the objects, and you can move them around on the screen. Using VPLAYER, you can also resize the viewports, freeze layers and hide lines in each viewport separately when plotting. Once you have them the way you want them, you can plot all the viewports out exactly as they're arranged onscreen.

Now, let's go back to the poster board metaphor. The various items are positioned, but you want to draw on the poster board itself in order to label items on your model and maybe even draw arrows from one item to another. But after you've drawn these labels on the poster board, what would happen if the items themselves were moved? Obviously, the items and labels would not match.

Remember, when you're in MSPACE, you're actually working on the model within the viewport. When you're in PSPACE, you're working on the poster board, which allows you to draw on the background and move the viewport objects around. This is the equivalent of being able to draw on the poster board itself. Once everything is exactly the way you want it, you can plot it all out at once from Paper Space. The really nice thing about this is that when you return to TILEMODE 1 (the original Model Space), everything you drew on the background in TILEMODE 0 (the poster board) is left behind until you return to Paper Space.

Have you ever wanted to have two drawings in memory at one time and be able to toggle between them? This can be a real productivity booster, and it's now possible.

One of the things you need to remember with Paper Space is that you don't have to create any viewports in order to use it. When you first change TILEMODE to 0, your screen should go blank, assuming you haven't created any viewports (the original model will not be visible in Paper Space until you create at least one viewport). Remember also that you can draw directly on the poster board. So, what if you inserted another drawing at 0,0 on the blank screen in Paper Space? It would be visible in this mode of your drawing without in any way affecting the original model in Model Space. This is the equivalent of having two drawings in memory at one time. You can toggle between them just as you would with a word processing document, by switching from TILEMODE 1 to TILEMODE 0.

If you need to copy or move information from one drawing to another, use WBLOCK and INSERT. This is the same as blocking, cutting and pasting in word processing. As far as AutoCAD is concerned, these two drawings are completely separate and can be plotted separately. Just begin your plot either in TILEMODE 1 or TILEMODE 0. There's one other benefit in the Paper Space mode: you can create a little viewport "window" of the other drawing using the MVIEW command. This gives you your own birds-eye view without needing a display-list processing card or software in your machine.

Reference Files

External Reference (XREF) is a feature that lets you use an external drawing as a block without including it in the existing drawing. There are several advantages to this technique. First, you can save an enormous amount of disk space. Instead of a large, space-consuming drawing becoming part of a drawing file, the drawing is made into a DWG block file that can be referenced when needed by any number of other drawings. Second, any changes to the original block or base external file are automatically reflected in every drawing file that references it.

An easy way to understand External Reference is to compare it to font shape files. The font shape doesn't actually reside in each drawing; it's only *referenced* in each drawing. Therefore, the font shape file must be on disk each time the drawing is brought up. If AutoCAD can't find the proper font file, it asks you to supply the name of another. The same applies to External Reference files—they must exist on disk where AutoCAD can find them each time they're called for.

At any time after you've inserted a drawing as a reference file, you can make the external file a block within the drawing.

External Reference files can't be changed in any way within the drawing file; they must be changed or edited within their own files. If you make changes directly to an External Reference file, nothing special has to be done for those changes to be reflected in any drawing files that reference it.

More Productivity With GRIPS

GRIPS is a feature that for some reason is not used that much by most users. That's a shame, since it can save a lot of time once you get into the habit of using it. GRIPS provides control points without having to use OSNAP or certain AutoCAD commands (such as the five GRIPS options listed below). Grips are used as fast-base access points for AutoCAD objects. The following GRIP options can be called: STRETCH, MOVE, ROTATE, SCALE or MIRROR. Remember, to function, GRIPS must be enabled.

Grips are control boxes that appear on objects. They are located at different sites, depending on the kind of object. For example, on lines, they appear at the endpoint and the midpoint. On circles, they appear at the center and the quadrants. On polylines, they appear at the vertices. And on text and blocks, they appear at the insertion point.

Enabling Grips

First and foremost, grips must be enabled. You do this through the Grips dialog box (see Figure 13-9) or the GRIPS system variable. (Enter **DDGRIPS** from the command line or select Grips from the Settings pull-down menu. Then check either or both of the check boxes to enable grips and/or grips within blocks.)

Figure 13-9: The Grips dialog box.

Second, you must be using Noun/Verb Selection mode, which is selected through the Object Selection Settings dialog box. (See Figure 13-10.) You know if you're using Noun/Verb, because a pick box is always available at the intersection of your crosshairs.

Figure 13-10: The Object Selection Settings dialog box.

There are two types of grips: those that simply show where the grips are and those that show that a grip has been selected. In the Grips dialog box, pick either the Unselected button or the Selected button, and a color map appears. Pick any color, and that will be the color used for the grips.

At the bottom of the Grips dialog box is a slide bar labeled Min and Max. To the right is a picture of the actual size of the grip. Move the slide bar to the left or right and see the size of the grip change. When the grip is the correct size, OK the dialog box.

Activating Grips

To activate a grip, all that's necessary is to pick an object. Then the grips appear. (Esc will generally turn them off.) Begin by picking one or more objects before you enter a command. The grips will appear. Pick any grip; notice that, as you get close to it, you're snapped to the grip. Once a grip is picked, it turns colors to identify that a base point has been selected.

Grips are used as a quick base point for the following commands: STRETCH, MOVE, ROTATE, SCALE and MIRROR.

Stretching With Grips

Once you've selected a base point, you're automatically in the Stretch mode. (This is a slight misstatement, since the only thing you're stretching is the point where the grip lies.) If the object you're working with happens to be a line, and the base point is the midpoint, simply pick another place on the screen, and the entire line moves. If the base point is the endpoint of the line, pick another point on the screen, and the endpoint of the line moves, "stretching" the line to that point and at that angle.

So, as you can see, each base point you pick has a different result. Generally, if you pick the midpoint of a line or the center of a circle or the insertion point of text or block, Stretch has the ability to move the circle or line.

Copying With Grips

To copy using grips, begin by picking one or more objects before you enter a command. The grips will then appear. Pick any grip. This is the base point.

Before you pick the next point on the screen, hold down the Shift key. Now the object is copied rather than moved. By picking another point, you're automatically in a multiple copy mode. This copying will continue until you press Enter.

You can copy and offset a fixed distance using grips. Begin by picking one or more objects before you enter a command. The grips will appear. Pick any grip. This is the base point.

Before you pick the next point on the screen, hold down the Shift key. Now the object is copied to the new point. Continue to hold down the Shift key, and point to another approximate location. Not only is the object copied to that location, but it's automatically copied the same distance as the original offset from the base point. The snap increments are thus set to the same offset.

Moving Objects With Grips

There are two ways to move objects using grips. Begin by picking one or more objects before you enter a command. The grips will appear. Pick any grip. This is the base point.

You are automatically in the Stretch mode. Therefore you must shift to the Move mode. Do this by entering **MO** or by picking MOve from the side screen menu. You can also toggle through the options by Enter or the spacebar.

Remember that you can move an object by picking the center or mid-point while in the Stretch mode, and the entire object will move. The Move mode, on the other hand, will permit you to use any base point and will move the object.

If you need to move and copy, begin by picking one or more objects before you enter a command. The grips will appear. Pick any grip. This is the base point.

This is a combination of copying (remember to hold the Shift key down when you pick the second point) and moving. Begin by picking the base point. Then pick MOve. Now, before you pick the second point, hold the Shift key down, and the object will be copied instead of moved.

You could do this with STRETCH, but only if the base point were the midpoint or the center. Otherwise, it will copy at the stretched angle, depending on which base point is picked.

Rotating With Grips

To rotate using grips, begin by picking one or more objects before you enter a command. The grips will appear. Pick any grip. This is the base point.

Enter **RO** or pick ROtate from the side screen menu. You can also toggle through the options by using Enter or the spacebar. The object will then rotate around the base point.

Scaling With Grips

Scaling is done in a similar manner. Begin by picking one or more objects before you enter a command. The grips will appear. Pick any grip. This is the base point.

Enter **SC** or pick SCale from the side screen menu. You can also toggle through the options by using Enter or the spacebar. The object will then be scaled relative to the base point.

Mirroring With Grips

Mirroring using grips works in a similar manner, but can be tricky if you want the original image to remain. Begin by picking one or more objects before you enter a command. The grips will appear. Pick any grip. This is the base point.

Enter **MI** or pick MIrror from the side screen menu. You can also toggle through the options by using Enter or the spacebar. The object will use the base point as the beginning of the mirror line. If you pick the second point, the object will be mirrored and the first object erased. If you hold the Shift key down, the object will be mirrored, but the first object will not be erased.

Moving On

AutoCAD often provides more than one way to accomplish a given task. But as you've seen in this chapter, it usually happens that one method is more efficient than the others. You'll reach your maximum productivity when you discover which methods are best-suited to the tasks you need to accomplish, and then stick with those methods consistently.

I can't emphasize enough the importance of consistent standards and procedures, and their impact on applications of Computer Aided Design. Conventions need to be set up for layers, linetypes, colors, polyline weight, file names, VPORT configurations for modeling, etc. Procedures and rules need to be developed for the creation of files both in file names themselves and in directory path names, as well as for the use of "proto-type" drawings.

Layer standards become even more critical with the use of XREF reference files. If a part drawing is XREFed into the main drawing, you may not want to show the detailing, border, etc. You may want to have hidden lines turned off, or have some other features optionally shown. If every operator who creates a part file specifies the layers he or she wants, the operator creating or maintaining the file will have nightmares trying to figure out which layers need to be frozen. However, if all profile lines appear on the layers PROF1, PROF2 and PROF3 in all drawings, the drawing is easily understood and controlled.

With each new AutoCAD version, more sophistication and new problems require each company to make sure that its own standards and procedures accommodate the changing technology.

In the next chapter you will begin to learn the basics of working with the most productive system of them all, dialog boxes. This is almost a programming language in and of itself. In addition it requires a firm knowledge of AutoLISP to make it work.

14

How to
Program
Dialog Boxes

How to Program Dialog Boxes

Of all the customizing tools designed to enhance AutoCAD's productivity, the most dynamic to use is the dialog box. Until Release 12, all dialog boxes were hard-coded as part of the AutoCAD core program. Now you can create your own.

Before we begin with the particulars of how a dialog box is created, let's discuss the why's and when's. AutoCAD has done an excellent job of creating nearly all the basic dialog boxes you might need for the ordinary AutoCAD commands. So why would you want to create any new ones?

Let's begin by pointing out when a dialog box *isn't* really called for. First, it should never be used simply as a menu system. You'd be ill-advised to make the 10 or 12 AutoLISP programs you may have written part of your dialog box selection. The existing system of menu selections—offering pull-downs, cursor menus, images, toolbars and so forth—is more than adequate to handle that type of function efficiently and easily. To use a dialog box this way wouldn't bolster your productivity appreciably.

Dialog boxes become valuable when you need interactivity between the program and the user. This is especially true when you have several choices to make—like how many settings to use. The perfect time to create a dialog box, for example, is when your AutoLISP program needs to ask a series of prompts. It's much easier to select items from a dialog box than to answer questions at the command line. The beauty of a dialog box is that the user is free to choose items and make selections in a random order, uncontrolled by the program.

Unlike other customization methods in this book, successfully writing dialog boxes depends on your knowledge of AutoLISP. A dialog box is much more than just a selection of items. It's actually a graphical interface to an AutoLISP program. (We use the term AutoLISP here only for the sake of simplicity; an ADS program is equally applicable.)

Therefore, the instructions on the creation and implementation of dialog boxes will presume a basic knowledge of AutoLISP. The easiest way to learn AutoLISP is through a book like *AutoLISP in Plain English* (also from Ventana Press).

The concepts and rules of writing and interfacing with dialog boxes aren't difficult once you get a thorough understanding of the basic principles. Unfortunately, the source of most of your reference information, the *AutoCAD Customization Guide*, is neither thorough nor complete. In fact, to someone not familiar with programming in C, it can be downright cryptic. That's why this chapter is going to be invaluable to you.

It's not the purpose of this chapter to teach you everything you'll ever need to know about writing dialog boxes. (That could warrant a book in and of itself.) Instead, our purpose is to give you an understanding of the basics. And we're going to do this through detailed examples and explanations. By the time you're through with this chapter, you should be prepared to read the *Customization Guide* and begin to understand what it is saying. So let's get started.

First Simple Dialog Box

A dialog box requires two files. Generally, to save your sanity, they should have the same name. The first file is a text file describing the dialog box itself; this file will always carry the extension .DCL. The second file is the AutoLISP file (or ADS program), which not only activates and controls the dialog box but also contains other programming logic as needed. Of course, all AutoLISP files will have the extension .LSP.

Let's start by looking at a very simple dialog box and a very simple AutoLISP program, and then take things apart. Begin by creating the following two files as text files. First create the file TEST1.DCL:

```
test1     : dialog {
              label = "Test 1 Dialog Box";
          : edit_box {
                label = "Enter Text:";
                key = "tname";
          }
          ok_cancel;
          }
```

Now create the second file, TEST1.LSP:

```
(defun C:test1 ()
 (setq num (load_dialog "test1"))
```

```
  (new_dialog "test1" num)
  (mode_tile "tname" 2)
  (action_tile "accept" "(do_txt)(done_dialog)")
  (start_dialog)
  (unload_dialog num)
)
(defun do_txt ()
  (setq txt1 (get_tile "tname"))
)
```

It looks complicated, doesn't it? Actually, this one isn't so bad. But, characteristically, this procedure does take several lines to do even the simplest of things. All this dialog box does is to bring up a text box, where you can type something and thereby assign it to the AutoLISP variable txt1. Let's see what all this does.

How Does the .DCL File Work?
Let's begin with the TEST1.DCL file. This is the dialog description itself.

```
test1    : dialog {
```

This begins the name and description of the dialog box. (The name of the file and the name of the dialog box don't have to be the same, although it's more convenient if they are.) Therefore, the first thing in the .DCL file is the name of the dialog box. In this case it's test1.

```
: dialog {
```

A term we'll use over and over again is *DCL tile*. Everything in a dialog box is called a DCL tile. Even the dialog box itself is a DCL tile. DCL tiles may have parameters that describe how they work. Dialog tiles always begin with a : if there are other parameters. The first required DCL tile is called dialog, and it must have additional parameters. Those additional parameters are the rest of the dialog box. The additional parameters are always introduced by a {.

```
label = "Test 1 Dialog Box";
```

This is the first parameter of dialog. It's called label, and is set equal to "Test 1 Dialog Box". Each individual parameter must end with a semicolon. The label parameter of the dialog tile will be the title that will print at the top of the dialog box.

```
: edit_box {
```

Although everything that follows dialog is a parameter of the dialog tile, you can also have DCL tiles within DCL tiles. edit_box is a DCL tile. Since it has its own parameters, it will begin with a colon and introduce those parameters with a {. The edit_box DCL tile draws a box in which you can type text.

```
label = "Enter Text:";
```

This is the label of the edit_box. "Enter Text:" will be the prompt outside the text box. Notice that it ends with a semicolon because it's a parameter within a DCL tile.

```
key = "tname";
```

The key is also a parameter within edit_box. It is the unique name that you give a tile. In your AutoLISP program, this will be how you'll identify the specific tile. This particular key is called "tname". Notice that it must be in quotes. What you put in the quotes is up to you.

```
}
```

This ends the edit_box tile. Remember that the parameters began with a {. Therefore they end with a }. Edit_box had two parameters: label and key.

```
ok_cancel;
```

This is a DCL tile just as edit_box was a DCL tile. There is a big difference here. ok_cancel doesn't have any parameters. Therefore, it doesn't begin with a colon and doesn't have a {. But it does terminate with a semicolon.

```
}
```

This is the last }. It closes the : dialog { tile that began the dialog box.

If you're confused at this point, don't worry. There's a lot more explaining to come. And it will start making sense when we look at the AutoLISP side of working with dialog boxes. So let's look now at the TEST1.LSP file.

How Does the .LSP File Work?

Remember, it takes two files to make a dialog work. We just looked at one half, the .DCL file. Let's see what the other one does. This is the TEST1.LSP companion file.

```
(defun C:test1 ()
```

The first line defines the AutoLISP function the same as any AutoLISP function. This one is called TEST1. It has a C: prefix that will permit you to run the program (or dialog box) by entering **test1** just as you would any AutoCAD command.

```
(setq num (load_dialog "test1"))
```

(load_dialog) is a dialog-specific AutoLISP command. "test1" is the dialog box that is loaded. This must be the name of the file. It's not the name of the dialog box itself (though giving the file and the dialog box the same name will make things easier). When the .DCL file is loaded successfully, a unique ID number is returned. This ID number is assigned to the variable num. Shortly, you'll use this number to begin the dialog.

```
(new_dialog "test1" num)
```

(new_dialog) is a dialog-specific AutoLISP command. This is the command that brings the dialog box to the screen. It has two parameters: the name of the dialog box and the ID number. Remember, the name of the dialog box is the name you gave it before—: dialog {—in the .DCL file, not the name of the .DCL file itself. Do you see why it helps things if the .DCL file and the name of the dialog box are the same? Also, remember that (new_dialog) only brings the dialog box to the screen; it doesn't actually activate the tiles of the dialog box.

```
(mode_tile "tname" 2)
```

(mode_tile) is a dialog-specific AutoLISP command that controls the mode of a specific tile. The following are the values you can give to (mode_tile):

Value	Mode
0	Enable tile
1	Disable tile
2	Set focus to the tile
3	Select edit box contents
4	Flip image highlighting on or off

Here we've set the tile called "tname" to 2. This will set the initial focus to the text box tile. "tname" is the name we gave to the key for the edit_box tile.

```
(action_tile "accept" "(do_txt)(done_dialog)")
```

This is a complex line that needs a little background explanation. ok_cancel is a tile that has a key called "accept". Remember, all tiles that can be accessed by the user should have a key. We'll see shortly how we know that the key to ok_cancel is "accept". Just take my word for it now.

(action_tile) is a dialog-specific AutoLISP command that tells AutoLISP what to do when the tile indicated is selected. The parameters of (action_tile) are the key and the AutoLISP functions that are to be performed. Both the key and the AutoLISP functions must be in quotes. Therefore, "accept" is the key and "(do_txt)(done_dialog)" are the two things that are to be done when the OK button is activated: perform (do_txt) when OK is picked, followed by (done_dialog).

It's important that you also include (done_dialog) with the "accept" key (action_tile) in order to terminate the dialog. If you fail to do so, the dialog box will continue to be on the screen. You can of course remove the dialog box from the screen with the Cancel button, but the (do_txt) assignment will have taken place. Even though this will work, it will thoroughly confuse you. By the way, if you fail to put an ok_cancel or other exit button in your .DCL file, there will be no way to exit the dialog box. The user will have to reboot the computer in order to get out.

(do_txt) is not a dialog-specific AutoLISP command. It's a function that we wrote. You can see it at the end of the file. It simply sets the value we type into the edit_box to the AutoLISP variable txt1. So, when the OK button is picked, whatever is in the edit_box will be assigned to txt1.

Note: When you're working with AutoLISP programs that are controlling dialog boxes, it's really a good idea to write many little AutoLISP
functions within the file that can be called as subroutines rather than to try
to write a top-down design. That's because, with a dialog box, you have
no control over the order in which things are selected. This lends itself to a
more subroutine-oriented approach. That way, a subroutine is generally
attached to each of the tiles as required. (do_txt) is one such routine.

```
(start_dialog)
```

This is a dialog-specific AutoLISP command. (load_dialog) loads a file
into memory and returns an ID handle. (new_dialog) brings the dialog
box to the screen by using the parameters of the name of the dialog and
the ID handle that was returned. Even though it's on the screen, it's not
yet active. (start_dialog) begins the current dialog box in memory. At this
point the tiles are active.

```
(unload_dialog num)
```

When the dialog box terminates, it has only been removed from the
screen. It can be called back at any time by (new_dialog "test1" num),
assuming that the variable num is the correct ID handle. As such, you can
begin inadvertently stacking dialog boxes if you don't unload the dialog
box when you're through. That's what the (unload_dialog) AutoLISP
command does. Its only parameter is the ID handle for the dialog box that
you're unloading.

It's conceivable that you don't want to unload the dialog box; you only
want to hide it as you bring up another dialog box in its place. Then the
second dialog box could be unloaded and the first reactivated. At the end
of the program, the first should also be unloaded. If you use this procedure, be sure to use two different variables for the ID handle when you
use the (load_dialog) function for each dialog.

```
)
```

This is the closing parenthesis that ends the main function.

```
(defun do_txt ())
```

This defines the function (subroutine) called (do_txt).

```
(setq txt1 (get_tile "tname"))
```

(get_tile) is a dialog-specific AutoLISP command that returns the value of a specific tile at run time. It has one parameter that is the key of the tile from which you want the value. The key is a string. In the above line the value of the tile called "tname" is then assigned to the variable txt1.

```
)
```

This closes the (do_txt) function.

Here you have the minimum of what it takes to produce a simple dialog box. Although there are a lot of lines in these two files, you can see that the programs really aren't that difficult when broken down into their component parts.

Let's Run It

Now that we've written and explained our short, first dialog box, let's run it and see how it works. Remember that TEST1.LSP is the controlling AutoLISP file for the dialog box. It needs to be loaded and run first.

Type: `(load "test1") <Enter>`

This loads the AutoLISP program. You don't need to load the .DCL file, because your AutoLISP program will do that for you.

Type: `test1 <Enter>`

This begins the AutoLISP program, and the dialog box should appear. It should look like Figure 14-1.

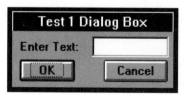

Figure 14-1: Test 1 dialog box.

Now type something in the text box. Notice that the vertical bar is already blinking. You don't have to first pick the text box. This was caused by the (mode_tile) command set to 2. This caused the initial focus to be on the text box. *Focus* means to activate a tile as though you had picked it. It's immediately ready for you to type.

When you've finished typing, press Enter. You'll notice that nothing happens. Pick the OK button. Now the dialog box disappears as you expected.

Let's see what is now in our variable txt1.

Type: `!txt1 <Enter>`

What you typed in should now appear at the command line in quotes. This proves that the dialog box works and that what was typed in is now assigned to the variable txt1.

Why do you suppose we weren't able to press Enter while in the text box, and have the OK button as the default, as it is on many dialog boxes? Well, you can, but you have to tell the dialog box what you want it to do. When most other tiles have the focus, the OK is usually accepted as the default. This means that Enter is the same as picking the OK button. But an edit_box is different. When it has the focus, Enter will not activate the OK button unless you permit it. The way to permit it is to add the following as one of the attributes of the specific edit_box:

`allow_accept = true;`

Change the TEST1.DCL file to reflect this change. The TEST1.DCL file should now look as follows:

```
test1     : dialog {
              label = "Test 1 Dialog Box";
          : edit_box {
              label = "Enter Text:";
              key = "tname";
              allow_accept = true;
              }
          ok_cancel;
          }
```

You've now given permission for the user to use Enter to OK the dialog box while the edit_box has the focus.

Parts of a Dialog Box

Now that you've written your first dialog box, let's look in more detail at how the .DCL file itself is put together and what many of your options are.

At Our Disposal

button   Any box that can be picked. Generally, when a button is picked, an action occurs. An example is the OK button.

radio_button   One of a group of buttons resembling the buttons on a car radio. Only one button in the group can be active at a time. When you press a button on your car radio, one station is tuned in. Likewise, when you activate one radio button in AutoCAD, the other buttons in the group deactivate.

toggle   This appears as a box with or without an X in it. When the toggle picked the first time, the X appears. When it's picked again, the X disappears. Therefore, it's acting as an off/on switch.

image   A rectangle with a graphic. This graphic can be an icon or a color.

image_button   This displays an image, but you can pick it as a button. This means that it has a graphic rather than a label (text).

text   This tile can't be activated. It simply causes text to appear on the dialog box. This shouldn't be confused with a label attribute, which we'll discuss later in this chapter.

edit_box   A tile where text can be typed in by the user. For example, we used an edit_box in our TEST1.DCL sample program.

list_box   Contains a list of text strings. The user is able to select from the list. If the list is too long for the box, you can use a scroll bar to display additional items. Only one item in a list can be selected at a time.

popup_list   The popup_list and the list_box are similar. The list_box is always visible in its entirety. The popup_list is displayed only as a single button until it is chosen. You know a popup_list because it has a down arrow beside the label. When it's picked, the list pops up. When the item is chosen, the list retracts.

slider   Obtains a numeric value by dragging the slider indicator.

spacer   This tile actually doesn't show, but is used to force space between other tiles.

Layouts of the Previous Tiles

column   This is not a tile in and of itself, since it can't be picked. Only the individual tiles within the column can be selected. It's a designation of the layout of the subsequent tiles used as parameters. The tiles are laid out vertically.

row   Similar to the column in terms of its function, except that the tiles are horizontal.

boxed_column   Same as a column except that there's a box around it.

boxed_row   Same as a row except that there's a box around it.

radio_column   A column with radio_buttons.

radio_row   A row with radio_buttons.

boxed_radio_column   A radio_column with a box around it.

boxed_radio_row   A radio_row with a box around it.

Tile Attributes

Now that you've seen some of the kinds of DCL tiles that are available, let's switch our attention to attributes. An attribute helps to further define a tile. Look at the following from our TEST1.DCL example:

```
: edit_box {
  label = "Enter Text:";
  key = "tname";
  allow_accept = true;
  }
```

label, key and allow_accept are all attributes. label tells what title to print next to the text box. key is the name by which your AutoLISP program knows this specific tile. You see you could have several edit_boxes in the .DCL file. Each edit_box would have a different key name. Allow_accept is an attribute that is either true or false. True and false are known as keywords (not to be confused with the key). If this particular attribute is true, it will allow the Enter to be an OK. If it's false, it will not allow the Enter to be the OK.

Another important attribute is value. This is what the tile contains. Naturally, the meaning of a tile's value is different, depending on the tile. Look at the final line added to the edit_box below:

```
: edit_box {
  label = "Enter Text:";
  key = "tname";
  allow_accept = true;
  value = "Starting Text Goes Here";
  }
```

The initial edit_box would have a line of text already in it, saying "Starting Text Goes Here." This would remain the value of the edit_box until you changed it at run time. Add this line to your TEST1.DCL file and see what happens. (See Figure 14-2.) Notice that the phrase Starting Text Goes Here tries to appear in the edit_box, but doesn't quite fit. This doesn't change the fact that the edit_box tile still has Starting Text Goes Here as its value. If you OK the box without changing it and type **!txt1**, you'll see that the AutoLISP variable txt1 now has the value of Starting Text Goes Here.

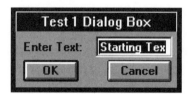

Figure 14-2: Test 1 dialog box with attributes.

Let's add another attribute to the edit_box. This is the width attribute.

```
: edit_box {
  label = "Enter Text:";
  key = "tname";
  allow_accept = true;
  value = "Starting Text Goes Here";
  width = 40;
  }
```

Now run the dialog box. As you can see from Figure 14-3, the size or width of the edit_box has been expanded to 40 characters, which permits our default value to easily fit. Note that the exact size of width will be determined by the resolution with which the user is running. Therefore all dialog boxes should be checked at 640 x 480 resolution.

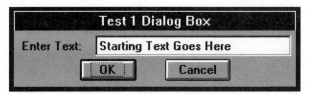

Figure 14-3: Test 1 dialog box with expanded width attribute.

This should give you an idea of what attributes do. Their effect is different on different tiles, and not all tiles can have the same attributes.

In the *AutoCAD Customization Guide* there is a complete list of all the available tiles and attributes, as well as what the attributes do. The following are some of the more common attributes and their meanings:

allow_accept   Available in the edit_box, image button and list_box. If true, it allows you to pick the OK button by pressing Enter.

edit_limit   Available in the edit_box. This is an integer that will limit the number of characters a user can enter.

height   Available in all tiles. This is the height of the tile.

fixed_width, fixed_height   These are available in all tiles. If you don't use these, the width and the height of the tile can change, depending on the layout of the dialog box. If these attributes are set to true, the width and/ or height of the tile doesn't change during the layout.

is_cancel   Available only for buttons. If a button is assigned this attribute, it is activated by a Ctrl+C or Esc, depending on the AutoCAD version and the operating system that you're using.

is_default   Available only for buttons. If a button is assigned this attribute, it is activated by pressing Enter. This is also platform dependent.

key   Available for all *active* tiles (that is, tiles that can be picked by the user). This is the name that the tile goes by for the application.

label   Available for all rows, columns, boxes, radio buttons, buttons, dialogs, edit_boxes, list_boxes, pop-up lists, texts and toggles. This generally is the displayed text as a title of the box or the displayed text within a button.

list   Available for list_box and pop-up list. These are the initial values to be displayed in the list.

mnemonic   Available for all *active* tiles (that is, tiles that can be picked by the user.) This attribute will cause an underscore to be displayed on the label and permit an Alt+letter to activate the tile. This is a keyboard shortcut. It is platform dependent.

value   Available for text and all active tiles except buttons and image buttons. This attribute sets the tile's initial value. (This is not to say that a button can't have a value. The value of a button is determined at run time.)

Dialog Definitions

To help you understand how tile definitions are put together, let's try a little experiment. Let's create a new file called USER.DCL:

```
spbox : edit_box {
  label = "Enter Text:";
  key = "tname";
  allow_accept = true;
  value = "Starting Text Goes Here";
  width=40;
  }
```

Now let's change TEST1.DCL to the following:

```
@include "user.dcl"
test1  : dialog {
     label = "Test 1 Dialog Box";
   spbox;
   ok_cancel;
   }
```

Notice that TEST1.DCL begins with @include "user.dcl". This tells AutoCAD to look in the file called USER.DCL for tile definitions. Remember that in USER.DCL we defined a tile of our own called spbox. We defined it as an edit_box with a label, key, allow_accept, value and width. We can now use that definition in any dialog box we create in the future as long as we include the USER.DCL file at the beginning. Then all we have to do is reference the new tile we created as spbox. Notice that our spbox does not have attributes. This is because our tile inherited the attributes from the edit_box in the USER.DCL file. If you run the new dialog box, you'll see that it runs the same.

This opens up some interesting possibilities. For example, ok_cancel isn't really a primitive tile. It's a tile that was created using other tiles and stored in a file called BASE.DCL. Let's look at how it was created. The following was taken from BASE.DCL, found in the AutoCAD SUPPORT directory. Let's look at what it took to create the simple ok_cancel.

First, a retirement_button was defined as follows:

```
retirement_button : button {
    fixed_width     = true;
    width           = 8;
    alignment = centered;
}
```

Next, an ok_button was defined as a retirement_button with the key set to "accept" and is_default set to true:

```
ok_button : retirement_button {
    label    = /*MSG1*/"  OK   ";
    key    = "accept";
    is_default = true;
}
```

Then, the cancel_button was defined as a retirement_button with the key set to "cancel" and is_cancel set to true:

```
cancel_button : retirement_button {
    label    = /*MSG3*/"Cancel";
    key    = "cancel";
    is_cancel= true;
}
```

Finally, it was all put together. It's a single column of a row of two buttons, the ok_button and the cancel_button. These are separated with a spacer with a width of 2. Notice that all of the attributes of the previously defined tiles are inherited by this single ok_cancel tile.

```
ok_cancel : column {
  : row {
    fixed_width = true;
    alignment = centered;
    ok_button;
```

```
         : spacer { width = 2; }
         cancel_button;
      }
   }
```

There are many of these predefined for you in BASE.DCL. Anything that is defined in BASE.DCL is automatically available to any other .DCL file. If you create your own USER.DCL type of file, it will need to be included in the dialog box .DCL file at the beginning of the file, as it was in our example.

Caution: It would be an error to modify the BASE.DCL file. If you make a mistake, you can make a mess of all other dialog boxes. Therefore, it would be best if an application created its own .DCL file to be included, if this becomes necessary.

There's another file used by the standard version of AutoCAD Release 13: ACAD.DCL. Don't touch this file. If you like what you see in this file, you can copy and paste the information to the USER.DCL file of your choice. Dialog boxes can't use the definitions of ACAD.DCL directly.

Now the syntax of the .DCL files should be easier to understand. Let's take a look at the rules. The tile definition may occur outside or inside the dialog box .DCL file. It has this format:

```
name : tile {
   attribute = value;
   attribute = value;
   attribute = value;
   }
```

For example,

```
spbox : edit_box {
   label = "Enter Text:";
   key = "tname";
   allow_accept = true;
   value = "Starting Text Goes Here";
   width = 40;
   }
```

spbox is defined outside our dialog box, TEST1.DCL. spbox is the name. This is followed by a colon and then the tile. If the tile has attributes, they're introduced with a {. Then the attributes of label, key, allow_accept, value and width follow. This is terminated by a }.

Once spbox has been defined either in the dialog box itself or in an external .DCL file, it can be referenced and used in other tile definitions. The format is as follows:

```
name;
```

This format can also be used. (Notice that it only needs the : and the {} when there are additional attributes.)

```
:name {
  attribute = value;
  }
```

If you want to include comments in the .DCL file, you can set them off with a //; for example,

```
/This is a comment/
```

A More Complex Dialog

Let's try a little more complicated dialog box and use what we've learned so far. This dialog box (.DCL) and accompanying AutoLISP program (.LSP) file are called CHENT. Therefore, we'll create a CHENT.DCL and a CHENT.LSP file. This dialog box will permit you to select, using radio buttons, either LINE, CIRCLE or POLYLINE. It also brings up the standard AutoCAD color selection dialog box and permits you to pick a color. When you OK the box, it will make all entities of the type you selected the color you selected.

For example, if you want all circles in your drawing to be green, you'll select CIRCLE from the radio button and the color green from the color dialog, and then OK the box.

First create the CHENT.DCL file:

```
chent : dialog  {
        label = "Change Entity Colors";
        : boxed_row {
         : radio_button {
           label = "Lines";
           key = "button1";
```

```
      }
    : radio_button {
      label = "Polylines";
      key = "button2";
    }
    : radio_button  {
      label = "Circles";
      key = "button3";
     }
    }
    : text {
      label = "Color of entities selected";
    }
    : row {
     : button {
       label = "Color...";
       key = "color1";
       fixed_width = true;
     }
     alignment = right;
     : text {
      key = "colortxt";
      width = 3;
      fixed_width = true;
      fixed_height = true;
     }
     : image {
       key = "color2";
       height = 1;
       width = 3;
       fixed_width = true;
       fixed_height = true;
     }
    }
    ok_cancel;
  }
```

Now create the CHENT.LSP file:

```
(defun c:chent ()
 (setq num (load_dialog "chent"))
 (new_dialog "chent" num)
 (set_tile "button1" "1")
 (setclrblk)
 (action_tile "color1" "(do_colors)")
 (action_tile "accept" "(do_getent)(done_dialog)")
 (start_dialog)
 (done_dialog)
 (if (/ = a nil)(do_change))
)

(defun do_getent ()
(if (= "1" (get_tile "button1")) (setq a (ssget "x" '((0 . "LINE")))))
(if (= "1" (get_tile "button2")) (setq a (ssget "x" '((0 . "POLYLINE")))))
(if (= "1" (get_tile "button3")) (setq a (ssget "x" '((0 ."CIRCLE")))))
)

(defun do_change ()
  (command "chprop" a "" "c" clr "")
)

(defun do_colors ()
  (setq clr (acad_colordlg 7))
  (setclrblk)
)

(defun setclrblk ()
  (if (= clr nil) (setq clr 7))
  (set_tile "colortxt" (itoa clr))
  (setq width (dimx_tile "color2"))
  (setq height (dimy_tile "color2"))
  (start_image "color2")
  (fill_image 0 0 width height clr)
  (end_image)
)
```

Before we dive into the explanation, try the dialog box to get the feel of how it works. Begin by drawing a series of circles, lines and polylines on the screen.

Type: `(load "chent") <Enter>`

Type: `chent <Enter>`

Response: (See Figure 14-4.)

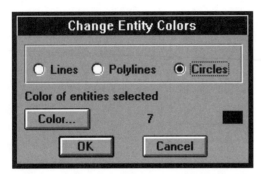

Figure 14-4: Change Entity Colors dialog box.

Now pick the Circles radio button. Pick the Colors button. Pick and OK any color. Now OK the dialog box. Notice that all the circles change to that color.

The CHENT.DCL File

I know this looks overwhelming, but let's take it in small chunks. We'll start with the .DCL file. It's the easier to understand.

```
chent : dialog  {
```

It begins with the name of the dialog called chent, followed by a colon and the tile dialog, which introduces the attributes with a {. Remember that the entire dialog box is really a single tile definition, therefore all the tiles in the dialog box act as attributes to dialog.

```
label = "Change Entity Colors";
```

This is the first attribute of dialog itself. This is what will appear in the title bar of the dialog box.

```
: boxed_row {
```

This is the next attribute of dialog. It's a boxed_row tile. Because the boxed_row has attributes, it begins with a colon and sets off the attributes with a {.

```
: radio_button {
  label = "Lines";
  key = "button1";
}
```

This is the first attribute of the boxed_row. It's a radio_button. This radio_button has two attributes. Its label is "Lines" and its key is "button1". Notice that each attribute ends with a semicolon. The radio_button terminates its attributes with a }.

```
:  radio_button {
   label = "Polylines";
   key = "button2";
 }
: radio_button  {
  label = "Circles";
  key = "button3";
 }
}
```

Just as with the first radio_button, there are two more radio_buttons under boxed_row. They have labels of "Polylines" and "Circles" and keys of "button2" and "button3". Each radio_button set of attributes terminates with a }. There is one additional } to terminate the boxed_row.

```
: text {
  label = "Color of entities selected";
}
```

This is the next attribute under dialog. It's a text area that has the label "Color of entities selected."

```
: row {
```

The file now begins a row.

```
: button {
 label = "Color...";
 key = "color1";
 fixed_width = true;
   }
```

The first attribute of the row is a simple button. Its label is "Color..." Notice the ellipses (...) in the label. This is a convention meaning when this button is picked, another dialog box will follow. The key for this button is "color1". The attribute fixed_width is true. We don't want the button to expand with the size of the row.

```
alignment = right;
```

This is a simple attribute under row. We want the row to be aligned to the right as opposed to left or center. Notice that, since this attribute doesn't have any attributes under it, it doesn't begin with a colon and doesn't have a {}.

```
: text {
   key = "colortxt";
   width = 3;
   fixed_width = true;
   fixed_height = true;
}
```

This group is an attribute under row. It's a text area that will carry the color number of the color that will eventually be selected. Its key is "colortxt", width is 3 and it has a fixed width and height.

```
: image {
   key = "color2";
   height = 1;
   width = 3;
   fixed_width = true;
   fixed_height = true;
}
```

This group is an attribute under row. It's an image rectangle. Its key is "color2". We have sized it as a 1 by 3 with a fixed size. The value of the image will be the color of the color we select at run time. As the value changes, the image will become the color we select.

```
}
```

This closes the row.

```
ok_cancel;
```

This is a referenced tile from BASE.DCL that places the OK and Cancel buttons. Remember that "accept" is the key for the OK portion of the tile.

```
    }
```

This closes the beginning dialog tile.

That wasn't so bad, was it? Now let's take a look at the AutoLISP side of the equation.

The CHENT.LSP File

The AutoLISP file, CHENT.LSP is divided into five functions:

- (c:chent) is the controlling function. This is the one that starts the program and the dialog box.
- (do_getent) is a function that checks to see which radio button was picked and does an (ssget) filter to select all the entities in the drawing that match the object type selected. These are collected as a selection set and assigned to the variable a.
- (do_change) issues the AutoCAD command CHPROP and changes the entities in the selection set to the color selected.
- (do_colors) is the function that calls the standard AutoCAD color dialog box so that the user can pick the color. The color picked is returned by the standard AutoCAD color dialog box and is assigned to the AutoLISP variable clr.

- (setclrblk) is the function that paints the image tile the color selected and places the color number in the text area.

Note: There is no magic in (do_ as a prefix. It's simply a made-up name for the function. Notice also that (c:chent) is the only one that has a c: prefix. This permits **CHENT** to be entered from the AutoCAD command line. Look at what each of the functions does.

Let's begin the explanation with (c:chent):

```
(defun c:chent ()
```

This defines the function as a command-level function called CHENT.

```
(setq num (load_dialog "chent"))
```

This loads the dialog file "chent" and returns the ID handle to the AutoLISP variable num.

```
(new_dialog "chent" num)
```

This brings the dialog box to the screen. "chent" is the name of the dialog tile, not the file. num is the ID handle.

```
(set_tile "button1" "1")
```

(set_tile) is a dialog-specific AutoLISP command that sets the value of a tile. The parameters of the command are the key of the tile to be set and the value it is to be set to. Both parameters are strings.

```
(setclrblk)
```

This function is run at this time to set a default color, if there is none, so that the image and text tiles will have something in them when the dialog box comes up. Since the variables used are global, they will inherit the previous selection to start with. If this is the first time, the variables are preset to color number 7.

```
(action_tile "color1" "(do_colors)")
```

(action_tile) is a dialog-specific AutoLISP command. It's activated by a concept known as a *callback*. This means that the (action_tile) puts Auto-

LISP on notice that, if a specific tile is picked, certain things are to happen. What specifically is to happen depends on what you put in the (action_tile) command.

The syntax for (action_tile) is (action_tile key action). key and action are strings. The key is the tile that's picked. The action is what will happen when the tile is picked. In the above case the key is "color1". This is the key for a button with the label "Colors..." The next parameter is the action. In this case it is "(do colors)". This seems like a strange syntax. (do_colors) is of course an AutoLISP function call. But notice that the entire function call is in quotes. This is because the parameters of key and action must both be strings.

```
(action_tile "accept" "(do_getent)(done_dialog)")
```

This is an (action_tile) for the key "accept". Do you remember which tile has the key "accept"? It's the OK button. How do you know this? In order to know this you would have had to look into the BASE.DCL file and trace the referenced tile ok_cancel back to its inherited attributes. There you would see that the tile called ok_button has a key "accept". Therefore, when the OK button is picked, the action is twofold: (do_getent) and (done_dialog). Note that both of these are within quotes, since the action must be a string.

Important: All (action_tile) commands must come *before* (start_dialog). This seems strange, but that's the way it is.

```
(start_dialog)
```

Remember that (new_dialog) only brings the dialog box to the screen. It doesn't actually activate any of the tiles. That's what (start_dialog) does.

```
(unload_dialog num)
```

This unloads the dialog from memory.

```
(if (/= a nil)(do_change))
```

After the dialog box leaves the screen, if the variable *a* isn't nil, the function (do_change) is called. This means that since (do_getent), which creates the selection set, is called only if the OK is picked, (do_change) will be called only if there's a selection set to change. Notice that (do_change) is called only after the dialog box leaves the screen. This is because certain AutoLISP commands can't be used while the dialog box is on the screen. One of these that can't be used is (command).

```
)
```

This closes the (c:chent) function.

```
(defun do_getent ()
(if (= "1" (get_tile "button1")) (setq a (ssget "x" '((0 ."LINE")))))
(if (= "1" (get_tile "button2")) (setq a (ssget "x" '((0 ."POLYLINE")))))
(if (= "1" (get_tile "button3")) (setq a (ssget "x" '((0 ."CIRCLE")))))
)
```

This is the (do_getent) function. It's a series of if statements testing the value of each of three tiles. Any time a radio button is picked, it's given the value of 1. If it's not picked, it has the value of 0. You can test for the value of a tile with the dialog-specific AutoLISP command (get_tile). It has only one parameter, and that is the key of the tile you're looking for. It returns the value as a string. Therefore, if "button1" is picked, then (setq a (ssget "x" '((0 . "LINE")))). This is the (ssget) filter command that selects only lines. If "button2" is picked, only polylines are selected; if "button3" is picked, only circles are selected and placed in the selection set called a.

```
(defun do_change ()
  (command "chprop" a "" "c" clr "")
)
```

(do_change) is a simple function that issues the CHPROP command and selects the contents of selection set a. "c" stands for color, and clr is the variable that contains the color number.

```
(defun do_colors ()
  (setq clr (acad_colordlg 7))
  (setclrblk)
)
```

(do_colors) issues the AutoLISP call for the standard color dialog box. This is really an ADS AutoLISP function that is described in the AutoLISP manual. (acad_colordlg) is an AutoLISP command that brings up the dialog box. It has one required parameter and that is the default color when the box comes up. It returns the color number of the color selected. This is assigned to the variable clr. After the color dialog box is called, (setclrblk) is called to set the image color and the text color number.

```
(defun setclrblk ()
  (if ( = clr nil) (setq clr 7))
  (set_tile "colortxt" (itoa clr))
  (setq width (dimx_tile "color2"))
  (setq height (dimy_tile "color2"))
  (start_image "color2")
  (fill_image 0 0 width height clr)
  (end_image)
)
```

(set_tile "colortxt" (itoa clr)) sets the value of the tile whose key is "colortxt" to the value of clr. (itoa) converts the string to an integer. This will print the color number in the text area.

Remember that image is a tile that can contain a graphic. But it doesn't know what kind of graphic it will contain. That's up to the AutoLISP program to supply. Our image tile has a key set to "color2". Before we can simply assign a color value to our image, we have to know the size of the image tile. We can secure the size with the AutoLISP commands (dimx_tile) and (dimy_tile). These AutoLISP commands require the key as their parameter. They return the length of the X and the length of the Y respectively. These are set to the variables height and width. These variable names are our own invention; they don't actually mean height and width. They only contain the X and Y value of the size of the image tile.

In order to activate the image tile on the screen, use the AutoLISP command (start_image). It uses the key of the image tile as its parameter as a string.

Finally, you have to fill the image with the color. Use (fill_image) to do this. It needs to know the beginning coordinate of the tile, the X value, the Y value and the color number. The 0 0 means begin at the beginning of the tile and fill a color the length of the X and the length of the Y, using the color number.

Before the color will actually appear, you must issue the AutoLISP command (end_image).

Moving On

The variations of how to build dialog boxes are of course infinite. This chapter was not meant to cover every possibility. In order to make these programs more readable and not confuse the issues with additional code, no error checking was done. A good programmer will want to put in a lot more "if" statements to see if files are loaded, required items picked, entries verified, etc. This will make the code more and more complex.

What we've hoped to do here is give an explanation of how dialog boxes are put together. With this explanation, you should be able to understand better the *AutoCAD Customization Guide.* It will seem difficult at first. Begin by writing your own small dialogs. Through the use of the explanations in this chapter and the AutoCAD reference guides, you'll begin to gain a deeper understanding as to how dialog boxes work.

Your introduction to a real AutoLISP application began in this chapter, where the first AutoLISP program file was applied as a graphical interface to a second .DCL text files, used to describe and create the simple dialog box. In the next chapter, you'll find 30 ready-to-run AutoLISP programs. These will take you a long way toward more applications and true AutoCAD productivity. On the companion disk at the back of this book you'll find all 30 files, plus bonus programs to help you work through the examples in this book.

15

The AutoCAD Productivity Library

The AutoCAD Productivity Library

One of the most productive things you can do for yourself is to learn Auto-LISP. AutoLISP is a productivity tool that comes free with every copy of AutoCAD. All you have to do is to learn how to use it. If you're not using AutoLISP, you're receiving only 70 percent of what you paid for.

This chapter contains 30 AutoLISP programs, ready to run. This is not intended to be a tutorial on writing AutoLISP programs. The purpose of these AutoLISP programs is to give you more productivity—immediately. Look through the programs to see what interests you. You may not use all of them this week or this month; but when you do need a specific AutoLISP program, it can be invaluable. (*AutoLISP in Plain English*, also from Ventana Press, is an excellent place to start learning AutoLISP. And for more information on how AutoLISP can help your productivity, see Appendix B.)

For each of these programs, use the following procedure to load and run the program. Each program has a name immediately following the function (defun. For example, the first AutoLISP program begins (defun C:cdist (). Therefore the name of the program is cdist.

To create the programs from scratch, the contents of each program should be typed into a text file. The actual name of the AutoLISP file is not important. It is assumed that the file will have the same name as the Auto-LISP program. For example, the first program is cdist and is found in CDIST.LSP. If you are using the disk included with this book, each of the programs will already be in its own file. This can save you a lot of time typing in programs, especially if you're not used to entering AutoLISP code.

Once the program has been typed, the file must be loaded before you can run the program. Using CDIST.LSP as an example, type the following from the AutoCAD command line:

Type: `(load "cdist") <Enter>`

Response: `C:cdist`

Once the file has been loaded, the program is available to run. For most of the programs, all you have to do is to type the name of the program to run it.

Type: `cdist <Enter>`

Cumulative Distances

Purpose: This program continuously measures points. Each time you pick another point, the program gives you the distance between the last two points and the cumulative distance of all points.

File Name: CDIST.LSP

Listing:
```
(defun C:cdist ()(graphscr)
    (setq d1 0)
    (setq pt1 (getpoint "\nPick the first point: "))
    (while (setq pt (getpoint "\nPick the next point: "))
    (setq d (distance pt1 pt))
    (setq d1 (+ d1 d))
    (prompt "\nDistance: ")(prompt (rtos d))
    (prompt "\nTotal Distance: ")(prompt (rtos d1))
    (setq pt1 pt)
    (setq pt nil)
    )
)
```

To Run:

Type: (load "cdist") <Enter>

Response: C:cdist

Type: cdist

Response: Pick the first point:

Pick the first point you want to measure. You may use any of your Object Snap options.

Response: Pick the next point:

Pick the second point you want to measure.

Response: (The program gives you both the distance between the two points and the total distance through that point. You may continue to pick points. When you have finished, press Enter and the program will terminate.)

Exploding Protected Blocks

Purpose: Sometimes blocks are purposely distorted slightly in order to protect them. As you'll recall, if a block is inserted with a different X and Y scale factor, you can't explode the block. And of course if you can't explode the block, then you can't edit it. Why would anyone do that on purpose in a drawing? It's done to prevent work from being used by others. But sometimes this gets in the way of legitimate editing of drawing parts. This program will return a block to its original XY scale factor, then explode it so it can be edited. (Note that beginning with Release 13, blocks with differing XY scale factors may be exploded with the regular AutoCAD EXPLODE command. If you don't have Release 13, this program is the only way it can be done. If you do have Release 13, it can still be very useful to use this program instead of the EXPLODE command because EXPLODE will maintain a small distortion. This program will correct the distortion.

To test out the program, create a block, then insert it with an X value of 1.0001 and a Y value of 1. The block will look all right, but it can't be exploded. Try it and see, then use xblock to explode the block.

By the way, this is a good technique if you want to keep someone from WBLOCKing your details out and using them. But as you can see, this works only for those who don't have a thorough understanding of Auto-CAD (or who haven't read or purchased this book).

File Name: XBLOCK.LSP

Listing:
```
(defun C:xblock  ()
   (setq a (entsel))
   (setq e (entget (car a)))
   (setq d (assoc 41 e))
   (setq d1 (assoc 43 e))
   (setq e (subst '(43 . 1) d1 e))
   (setq e (subst '(41 . 1) d e))
   (entmod e)
   (setq a1 (cdr a))
)
```

To Run:

Type: `(load "xblock") <Enter>`

Response: `C:xblock`

Type: `xblock <Enter>`

Response: `Select object:`

Pick the block. The block is now returned to its original state and can be exploded using the EXPLODE command so that it can be edited.

Autosave

Purpose: It's very important to save your drawing at predetermined periods of time. But sometimes we forget. This program will help remind you by automatically saving your drawing at your chosen intervals. AutoCAD has an automatic save feature controlled by a system variable called SAVETIME. The default value is set to 120 minutes. You can change it at any time to suit your drawing requirements by using the following simple procedure.

Type: `SETVAR`

Response: `Variable name or ?<.....>: SAVETIME`

Response: `New value for savetime <120>:`

Type: (Set it to any new value in minutes.)

AutoCAD users will find this program a more useful feature than the existing automatic save in AutoCAD. That's because most people misuse the autosave feature. In addition, the AutoCAD autosave does not preserve the backup. It is only temporary and can lead to disasters if it's not handled properly.

Our program is divided into three parts. The first part, C:SAVETIME, sets the interval of time and undefines the REDRAW command. The second part, C:REDRAW, replaces the REDRAW command with an AutoLISP (ASAVE) program that runs before redrawing the screen. The third program *is* the (ASAVE) program, which actually checks the time, then saves the drawing when necessary. If the interval is not sufficient, the drawing will not be saved.

To change the amount of time between saves, change the value in the following statement.

```
(setq stime 1)
```

The 1 sets the interval at one minute. If you want it set to 30 minutes, change the program to

```
(setq stime 30)
```

File Name: SAVETIME.LSP

Listing:
```
(defun c:savetime ()
   (setq stime 1)
   (setq stime (/ stime 1440.0))
   (command "undefine" "redraw")
)
(defun C:redraw ()
   (asave)
   (command ".redraw")
)
(defun asave ()
   (if (> (- (getvar "date") (getvar "tdupdate")) stime)
   (progn
   (princ "\nSaving file . . . ")
   (command "save" "")
   )
   )
)
```

To Run:

Type: (load "savetime") <Enter>

Type: SAVETIME <Enter>

This begins the program. After that, the program virtually runs itself. Once it's loaded, it will check the last time the drawing was saved and save if appropriate whenever you enter the (ASAVE) command. The trick is to enter the (ASAVE) command as often as possible. The easiest way to do that is to make the (ASAVE) command part of a command such as

REDRAW. To do this, you'll need to undefine the REDRAW command and substitute an AutoLISP program called C:REDRAW. This has been done for you in the listing above. Now every time you issue the REDRAW command, it will really be using the AutoLISP C:REDRAW program, which always begins with (ASAVE), thus checking to see if the drawing has been saved within the interval. If it hasn't, then the (ASAVE) program will save the drawing before redrawing the screen.

Menu Editor

Purpose: The purpose of this program is to give you an automatic way to change Tablet Area 1 of your TABLET menu from inside AutoCAD without going through a text editor. If you do use a tablet, this can save you some time.

File Name: EDMENU.LSP

Listing:
```
(defun c:edmenu ()
    (setq mnf nil)(setq mnfm nil)
    (princ "\n ")(princ "\n ")
    (prompt "\nEnter name of menu file to modify - Do NOT add .MNU "
    (setq mnfm (getstring))
    (setq mnf (strcat mnfm ".mnu"))
    (setq stexp (strcat "copy " mnf))
    (setq stexp (strcat stexp " mctmp.mnu"))
    (command "shell" stexp)
    (setq fo (open "mctmp.mnu" "r"))
    (setq fn (open mnf "w"))
    (setq kwd (getstring "\nWhich menu block? Ex: [A-5] "))
    (setq kwd (strcase kwd))
    (setq nu (strlen kwd))
    (setq exp (getstring 1 "\nExpression "))
    (princ "\n ")(prompt "\nUpdating menu file - Please Wait . . . ")
    (while (setq mni (read-line fo))
    (if (= (substr mni 1 nu) kwd)
    (setq mni (strcat (substr mni 1 nu) exp)))
    (write-line mni fn)
```

```
        )
        (close fo) (close fn)
        (command "menu" mnfm)
        (princ)
    )
```

To Run:

Type: (load "edmenu") <Enter>

You must now decide which square you want to use and what you want it to do for you. If you look at Tablet Area 1, you'll see that it's a grid of A–H vertically and 1–25 horizontally. Let's assume you want to use square G-1 and you want it to erase the last thing you drew.

Type: EDMENU <Enter>

Response: Enter name of menu file to modify — Do NOT add .MNU

Type: ACAD <Enter> (This is your menu file. You may also use DRIVE and PATH.)

Response: Which menu block? Ex: [A-5]

Type: [g-1] (You must put the brackets around the coordinates, but you don't have to use uppercase letters unless you're in a UNIX environment.)

Response: Expression

Type: ^C^C(command "erase" "L" "")

Response: Updating menu file - Please Wait . . .

The program copies your menu to a temporary file, and makes the changes to your real file. The menu is reloaded and recompiled, ready for your use. Your old menu is called MCTMP.MNU. If you need it back, you must rename it before you run the program again.

ZOOM Extents Without Regeneration

Purpose: This program is divided into two parts. Run the first program, called zes, to set your zoom extents, then use ze to zoom to those extents without a regeneration.

File Name: ZE.LSP

```
Listing:  (defun C:ZES  () (graphscr)
             (setq exmin (getvar "extmin"))
             (setq exmax (getvar "extmax"))
          )

          (defun C:ZE ()
             (command "zoom" "w" exmin exmax)
          )
```

Metric Conversion: Feet to Millimeters

Purpose: This program converts an entire drawing from feet and inches to millimeters. Not only is the drawing converted, but the Limits, Snap, Grid and all dimension variables are also converted. The label "mm" is added to the dimension text.

File Name: MMCONV.LSP

```
Listing:  (defun C:mmconv () (graphscr)
             (setq a (ssget "x"))
             (command "scale" a "" "0,0" "r" "1" "25.4")
             (setvar "lunits" 2)
             (setvar "luprec" 4)
             (setq gri (getvar "gridunit"))
             (setq sna (getvar "snapunit"))
             (setq grix (car gri))
             (setq griy (cadr gri))
             (setq snax (car sna))
             (setq snay (cadr sna))
             (setq grix (* grix 25.4))
             (setq griy (* griy 25.4))
             (setq snax (* snax 25.4))
             (setq snay (* snay 25.4))
             (setq gri (list grix griy))
             (setq sna (list snax snay))
             (setvar "gridunit" gri)
             (setvar "snapunit" sna)
             (setq lim (getvar "limmax"))
```

```
            (setq limx (car lim))
            (setq limy (cadr lim))
            (setq limx (* limx 25.4))
            (setq limy (* limy 25.4))
            (setq lim (list limx limy))
            (setvar "limmax" lim)
            (setq sca (getvar "dimscale"))
            (setq sca (* sca 25.4))
            (command "dim" "dimscale" sca ^c)
            (command "dim" "dimpost" "mm" ^c)
            (command "dim" "update" a "" ^c)
            (command "zoom" "a")
        )
```

To Run:

Type: `(load "mmconv") <Enter>`

Response: `C:mmconv`

Type: `MMCONV <Enter>`

The program is now automatic. The drawing is converted to milli-meters. You can use the following program to convert it back.

Metric Conversion: Millimeters to Feet

Purpose: This program converts an entire drawing from millimeters to feet and inches. Not only is the drawing converted, but the Limits, Snap, Grid and all dimension variables are also converted. The label "mm" is removed from the dimension text.

File Name: `FTCONV.LSP`

Listing:
```
(defun C:ftconv ()(GRAPHSCR)
    (setq a (ssget "x"))
    (command "scale" a "" "0,0" "r" "304.8" "12")
    (setvar "lunits" 4)
    (setvar "luprec" 4)
    (setq gri (getvar "gridunit"))
    (setq sna (getvar "snapunit"))
```

```
(setq grix (car gri))
(setq griy (cadr gri))
(setq snax (car sna))
(setq snay (cadr sna))
(setq grix (/ grix 25.4))
(setq griy (/ griy 25.4))
(setq snax (/ snax 25.4))
(setq snay (/ snay 25.4))
(setq gri (list grix griy))
(setq sna (list snax snay))
(setvar "gridunit" gri)
(setvar "snapunit" sna)
(setq lim (getvar "limmax"))
(setq limx (car lim))
(setq limy (cadr lim))
(setq limx (/ limx 25.4))
(setq limy (/ limy 25.4))
(setq lim (list limx limy))
(setvar "limmax" lim)
(setq sca (getvar "dimscale"))
(setq sca (/ sca 25.4))
(command "dim" "dimscale" sca ^c)
(command "dim" "dimpost" "." ^c)
(command "dim" "update" a "" ^c)
(command "zoom" "a")
)
```

To Run:

  Type: `(load "ftconv") <Enter>`

Response: `C:FTCONV`

  Type: `FTCONV <Enter>`

The program is now automatic. The drawing is converted to feet and inches. You can use the previous program to convert it back to millimeters.

Copy From Paper Space

Purpose: At the top of many AutoCAD users' wish lists is the ability to maintain two drawings in memory simultaneously and transfer objects between the two. This program makes it easy. Begin with one drawing in Model Space (that is, TILEMODE 1). Now shift to Paper Space (TILEMODE 0). The screen will go blank. Set Limits and Units for Paper Space the same as for Model Space. Now insert another drawing in Paper Space. You can place an * before the drawing name to make it come in already exploded.

Use the MVIEW command to create one window in Paper Space. At this point you have two drawings visible at one time. The Model Space drawing is visible in the viewport. The inserted drawing is visible on the Paper Space screen. This program takes any objects in the Paper Space drawing and copies them to the Model Space viewport, where they can be placed.

File Name: PSCOPY.LSP

Listing:
```
(defun C:pscopy ()
    (prompt "\nSelect objects to copy: ")
    (setq a (ssget))
    (setq pt1 (getpoint  "\nBasepoint: "))
    (if (= nil (findfile "xxtempxx.dwg"))
    (command "wblock" "xxtempxx" "" pt1 a "")
    (command "wblock" "xxtempxx" "y" "" pt1 a "")
    )
    (command "oops")
    (command "mspace")
    (command "insert" "*xxtempxx")
)
```

To Run:

Type: (load "pscopy") <Enter>

Response: C:PSCOPY

Type: PSCOPY <Enter>

Response: Select objects to copy:

Select the objects in Paper Space that you want copied and confirm.

Response: Basepoint:

Pick the base point of the object. You are now switched to Model Space and the UCS icon appears in the Model Space window. Pick the point where you'd like the objects to be placed. Notice that there's no dragging image, since no real block was created. The program could be modified by removing the * from in front of *xxtempxx in order to get AutoCAD to drag the image. But this creates a block in your drawing and might require that you explode the objects afterward.

As the program is written, it copies the objects to Model Space while leaving the objects you copied in Paper Space. If you want the objects removed as they're copied, then remove the (command "oops") line from the program, or place a semicolon at the beginning of that line to comment it out.

3D Dimensioning

Purpose: In 3D dimensioning, if the current UCS is not parallel with the object being dimensioned, there's a real problem; in fact, it's possible to create a totally erroneous dimension. The proper way to dimension an object in 3D is to change the UCS to UCS Entity, then rotate the UCS so that the X arrow is pointing in the direction you want the dimension text to go. This program does that for you. It's as simple as a regular dimension command and it returns you to your current UCS.

File Name: 3DDIM.LSP

Listing:
```
(defun C:3ddim ()
    (setq os (getvar "osmode"))
    (setq e (car (entsel)))
    (command "ucs" "e" e)
    (setvar "osmode" 33)
    (setq pt1 (getpoint "\nFirst point: "))
    (setq pt2 (getpoint "\nSecond point: "))
    (setvar "osmode" 0)
    (setq pt3 (getpoint "\nDimension line location: "))
```

```
(command "point" pt1)
(setq a (entlast))
(command "point" pt2)
(setq b (entlast))
(command "point" pt3)
(setq c (entlast))
(command "ucs" "3point" pt1 pt2 "")
(setq pt1 (cdr (assoc 10 (entget a))))
(setq pt2 (cdr (assoc 10 (entget b))))
(setq pt3 (cdr (assoc 10 (entget c))))
(setq pt1 (trans pt1 0 1))
(setq pt2 (trans pt2 0 1))
(setq pt3 (trans pt3 0 1))
(command "dim" "hor" pt1 pt2 pt3 "" ^c)
(command "erase" a b c "")
(command "ucs" "p")
(command "ucs" "p")
(setvar "osmode" os)
)
```

To Run:

Type: (load "3ddim") <Enter>

Response: C:3DDIM

Type: 3DDIM <Enter>

Response: Select objects:

Select the object to be dimensioned.

Response: First point:

Pick the first dimension point. You're switched to an Object Snap Intersection and Endpoint. It's important here to pick the first and second points in the direction you want your dimension text to go.

Response: Second point:

Pick the second dimension point.

Response: Dimension line location:

Pick where you want your dimension line to be. The program now dimensions the line, and you're returned to your previous settings.

Quick Change Property

Purpose: The CHANGE command is too cumbersome to be efficient. Beginning with Release 10, AutoCAD introduced a CHANGE Property command that takes you straight to the properties you want to select from. In Release 11, there's really no difference between CHPROP and the Properties options in CHANGE, whereas in Release 12 and 13 you have the option of using a dynamic dialog box. Now with DDEDIT there is less need to use the CHANGE command for editing text.

The program substitutes CHPROP for CHANGE, even though you enter **CHANGE** or pick CHANGE from a menu. With this little program there's no need to modify any of your menus to add this efficiency. If you really want to use the CHANGE command,

Type: .CHANGE <Enter> (Notice the . in front of the command.)

File Name: CHANGE.LSP

Listing: (command "undefine" "change")
   (defun C:change ()
   (command "chprop")
)

To Run:

Type: (load "change") <Enter>

Response: C:change

Once the program file is loaded, it's active. Nothing more needs to be done. Simply type CHANGE or pick it from any menu and the CHPROP command will be issued instead. Of course, the program could be placed in your ACAD.LSP file.

If you ever want to disengage the program,

Type: redefine <Enter> CHANGE <Enter>

Perspective View

Purpose: DVIEW lets you set a perspective view from within DVIEW, but this is often difficult to use and visualize. Sometimes it's easier to position yourself and the target from a plan view. By picking the target and camera and then giving each an elevation, you're brought quickly to the proper perspective view.

File Name: PERSPV.LSP

Listing:
```
(defun C:perspv () (graphscr)
     (setq capt (getpoint "\nPick the camera point: "))
     (setq tapt (getpoint  "\nPick the target point: " capt))
     (setq cael (getdist "\nEnter the camera elevation: "))
     (setq capt (list (car capt) (cadr capt) (+ cael (caddr capt))))
     (setq tael (getdist  "\nEnter the target elevation: "))
     (setq tapt (list (car tapt) (cadr tapt) (+ tael (caddr tapt))))
     (setq dis (distance capt tapt))
     (command "dview" "" "d" dis "po" tapt capt "")
)
```

To Run:

Type: (load "perspv") <Enter>

Response: C:perspv

Type: PERSPV <Enter>

Response: Pick the camera point:

Pick the appropriate camera point (see Figure 15-1).

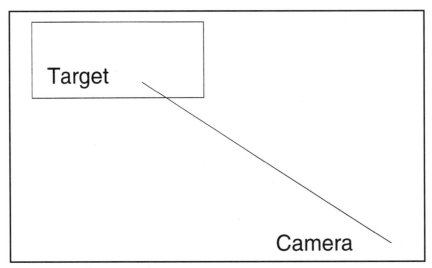

Figure 15-1: Camera and target points.

Response: Pick the target point:

Pick the appropriate target point (see Figure 15-1).

Response: Enter the camera elevation:

Type: 3' <Enter>

Response: Enter the target elevation:

Type: 20' <Enter>

Break Text

Purpose: AutoCAD has made great strides in the manipulation of text. But that doesn't mean there's no room for more tools for this purpose. This program searches for a text string within a text line and breaks the text at that point. The rest of the text that's been split off can then be placed anywhere you want it. Note that this program will work only for regular text objects, not MTEXT.

File Name: BRKTXT.LSP

Listing:
```
(defun C:brktxt (/ t d txt btxt tst len len1 e ct txtn txt2)
  (prompt "\nPick the line of text to break: ")
  (setq t (entget (car (entsel))))
  (setq d (assoc 1  t))
  (setq txt (cdr d))
  (setq btxt (getstring 1 "\nEnter sub-string to break: "))
  (setq tst (strcat "*" btxt "*"))
  (if (/= nil (wcmatch txt tst))
  (progn
  (setq len (strlen btxt))
  (setq len1 (- len 1))
  (setq e 1)
  (setq ct 1)
  (while e
  (if (= (substr txt ct len) btxt)
  (progn
  (setq txtn (substr txt 1 (+ ct len1)))
  (setq txt2 (substr txt (+ ct len)))
  (setq t (subst (cons 1 txtn) d t))
  (entmod t)
  (setq e nil)
  (setq t (subst (cons 1 txt2) (cons 1 txtn) t))
  (setq t (cdr t))
  (entmake t)
  (setq pt1 (cdr (assoc 10 t)))
  (command "move" "1" "" pt1 pause)
   )
  (setq ct (+ ct 1))
   )
   )
  ))
 )
```

To Run:

Type: (load "brktxt") <Enter>

Response: C:brktxt

Type: `BRKTXT <Enter>`

Start with a line of text such as "This is a very long line of text." Assume that the line is to be broken after the word "very," creating the following two lines:

```
This is a very
long line of text.
```

Response: `Enter sub-string to break:`

Type: `very <Enter>`

Remember to put one blank space after the word "very." That will begin the truncation of the line right before the word "long." The line will be broken, and you'll begin dragging the second half of the line into position. Pick the point, and the line is successfully split. Note this program will work only with regular text objects, not MTEXT.

Merge Text

Purpose: This assembles two lines of text into one.

File Name: MERGTXT.LSP

Listing:
```
(defun C:mergtxt ()
    (prompt "\nSelect first text to be merged: ")
    (setq e1 (entget (car (entsel))))
    (prompt "\nSelect second text to be merged: ")
    (setq e3 (car (entsel)))
    (setq e2 (entget e3))
    (setq d (assoc 1 e1))
    (setq tx1 (cdr d))
    (setq tx2 (cdr (assoc 1 e2)))
    (setq tx3 (strcat tx1 tx2))
    (setq e1 (subst (cons 1 tx3) d e1))
    (entmod e1)
    (command "erase" e3 "")
)
```

To Run:

Type:	(load "mergtxt") <Enter>
Response:	C:mergtxt
Type:	MERGTXT <Enter>
	Start with two lines of text.
Response:	Select first text to be merged:
	Pick the first line of text.
Response:	Select second text to be merged:
	Pick the second line of text. The two lines of text will be merged into one.

Bold Text

Purpose:	This program makes selected text bold by repeating the text and offsetting it slightly.
File Name:	BOLDTXT.LSP
Listing:	

```
(defun C:boldtxt ()
   (setq el (car (entsel)))
   (setq bf (getint "\nEnter BOLDNESS factor: "))
   (setq sf (getreal "\nEnter Scale factor: "))
   (setq sf (* 0.001 sf))
   (setq sf (strcat "@" (rtos sf) ",0"))
   (repeat bf
   (command "copy" el "" "@" sf)
   (setq el (entlast))
   )
)
```

To Run:

Type:	(load "boldtxt") <Enter>
Response:	C:boldtxt

Type: `BOLDTXT <Enter>`

>   Start with a line of text.

Response: `Enter BOLDNESS factor:`

>   The boldness factor is the number of times the line of text will be offset and repeated.

Type: `3 <Enter>`

Response: `Enter scale factor:`

>   The scale factor is the amount of offset. Whatever number you put in here will be multiplied by .001. Obviously the number you place here is dependent on the eventual scale you will plot.

Type: `96 <Enter>`

>   The line will be offset and repeated, thus giving it a bold appearance.

Change Text to Uppercase

Purpose: This program changes a line of text to uppercase. Note this program will work only with regular text objects, not MTEXT.

File Name: `CHCASEU.LSP`

Listing:
```
(defun C:chcaseu ()
   (prompt "\nPick a line of text: ")
   (setq e1 (entget (car (entsel))))
   (setq d (assoc 1 e1))
   (setq txt (cdr d))
   (setq txt (strcase txt))
   (setq e1 (subst (cons 1 txt) d e1))
   (entmod e1)
)
```

To Run:

Type: `(load "chcaseu") <Enter>`

Response: `C:chcaseu`

Type: `CHCASEU <Enter>`

Start with a line of text.

Response: `Pick a line of text:`

Pick a line of text and it will be changed to all uppercase.

Change Text to Lowercase

Purpose: This program changes a line of text to lowercase. Note this program will work only with regular text objects, not MTEXT.

File Name: `CHCASEL.LSP`

Listing:
```
(defun C:chcasel ()
    (prompt "\nPick a line of text: ")
    (setq e1 (entget (car (entsel))))
    (setq d (assoc 1 e1))
    (setq txt (cdr d))
    (setq txt (strcase txt 1))
    (setq e1 (subst (cons 1 txt) d e1))
    (entmod e1)
)
```

To Run:

Type: `(load "chcasel") <Enter>`

Response: `C:chcasel`

Type: `CHCASEL <Enter>`

Start with a line of text.

Response: `Pick a line of text:`

Pick a line of text and it will be changed to all lowercase.

Center Line of Circle

Purpose: This program draws a center line from the center of the circle to a point outside the circle.

File Name: CENPT.LSP

Listing:
```
(defun C:cenpt () (graphscr)
    (setq os (getvar  "osmode"))
    (setvar "osmode" 4)
    (setq pt1  (getpoint "\nSelect Circle: "))
    (setq pt2  (getdist pt1 "\nLength of center line: "))
    (setq d1  (strcat "@" (rtos pt2) "<<0"))
    (setq d2  (strcat "@" (rtos pt2) "<<90"))
    (setq d3  (strcat "@" (rtos pt2) "<<180"))
    (setq d4  (strcat "@" (rtos pt2) "<<270"))
    (command "line" pt1 d1 "")
    (command "line" pt1 d2 "")
    (command "line" pt1 d3 "")
    (command "line" pt1 d4 "")
    (setvar "osmode" os)
)
```

To Run:

Type: (load "cenpt") <Enter>

Response: C:cenpt

Type: CENPT <Enter>

Start with a circle.

Response: Select circle:

Pick the circle.

Response: Length of center line:

Enter the distance of the center line or point to the distance a little outside of the circle. You are tied to the center point of the circle to help you measure.

Attribute Builder

Purpose: This is not as much a ready-to-run program as it is an example of how a program can easily set up a series of attributes with defaults without going through the questions and manual setup involved with the ATTDEF command.

First let's assume you have three attributes you want to assign to a series of blocks with given defaults. These attributes may be Name, Cost and Color. Each of the blocks you're going to build will have the same attribute tags, but each will have different defaults.

File Name: ATTBLD.LSP

Listing:
```
(defun C:attbld ()
    (setq at1 "NAME")
    (setq at1a (getstring "\nDefault Name: "))
    (setq at2 "COST")
    (setq at2a (getstring "\nDefault Cost: "))
    (setq at3 "COLOR")
    (setq at3a (getstring "\nDefault Color: "))
    (command "attdef" " " at1 " " at1a pause pause "0")
    (command "attdef" " " at2 " " at2a " ")
    (command "attdef" " " at3 " " at3a " ")
)
```

To Run:

Type: (load "attbld") <Enter>

Response: C:attbld

Type: ATTBLD <Enter>

Begin with something you want to block with attributes.

Response: Default Name:

Type: XYZ Part <Enter>

Response: Default Cost:

Type: 3.50 <Enter>

Response: Default Color:

Type: Green <Enter>

Obviously, any answers would be proper. These are only examples of the tags you could have (the number of tags is unlimited). Notice that tag 1 is labeled AT1 and the default value is given to the variable AT1A. The second is AT2 and AT2A, respectively. This could go on and on for as many as you need, following this pattern. After the program is run, you'll still need to BLOCK or WBLOCK the part and the appropriate attributes.

UCS X

Purpose: When you're working in 3D, you often find the X arrow going in the wrong direction. This program lets you point to the direction of positive X, leaving the plane the same.

File Name: UCSX.LSP

Listing:
```
(defun c:ucsx ()
    (setq os (getvar "osmode"))
    (setvar "osmode" 33)
    (setq ptx (getpoint "\nDirection for X: "))
    (command "ucs" "3POINT" "" ptx "")
    (setvar "osmode" os)
)
```

To Run:

Type: (load "ucsx") <Enter>

Response: C:ucsx

Type: ucsx <Enter>

Begin with a 3D object. When requested, point to the direction of positive X. The program automatically sets your Object Snap to Endpoint/Intersection, then sets you back.

UCS Origin

Purpose: When working in 3D, often all you need to do is change the point of origin to place the UCS icon on the object or check to see if the UCS icon is going in the proper direction. With this program, you can pick a point on the object and the UCS icon will snap to the object at that point, assuming the UCSICON command is set to Origin.

File Name: UCSOR.LSP

Listing:
```
(defun C:ucsor ()
    (setq os (getvar "osmode"))
    (setvar "osmode" 33)
    (setq ptx (getpoint "\nPick the origin: "))
    (command "ucs" "origin" ptx)
    (setvar "osmode" os)
)
```

To Run:

Type: (load "ucsor") <Enter>

Response: C:ucsor

Type: UCSOR <Enter>

Begin with a 3D object. When requested, point to the origin and pick.

Selected Redraw

Purpose: When you're editing objects, sometimes they'll disappear because something was placed on top of them or parts of another object were erased. In such cases, a redraw could restore everything to normal. But why redraw the whole screen when you can put a window around the only area you want redrawn? With this method, only those objects will be refreshed, thus saving you some time.

File Name: REDR.LSP

Listing:
```
(defun C:redr ()
    (setq blm (getvar "blipmode"))
    (setvar "blipmode" 0)
    (setq a (ssget))
    (setq n (sslength a))
    (setq i 0)
    (repeat n
    (redraw (ssname a i) 1)
    (setq i (+ i 1))
    )
    (setvar "blipmode" blm)
)
```

To Run:

Type: (load "redr") <Enter>

Response: C:redr

Type: REDR <Enter>

Response: Select objects:

Place a window or crossing window around the affected area of the screen. Now confirm with Enter. The objects within the window or crossing window will be redrawn.

Permanent Spline

Purpose: A Spline curve or a curve-fitted polyline takes an enormous amount of regeneration time. In addition, there's always the risk of accidentally decurving the polyline, especially if you explode it. This program makes a Spline or curve-fitted polyline permanent with a single pick by turning it into joined polyline segments. *Note:* This program will work only on polyline objects, not Spline objects.

File Name: PERMSP.LSP

Listing:
```
(defun C:permsp ()
  (prompt "\nPick spline or fitted poly line: ")
  (setq e (entsel))
  (setq e1 (car e))
  (setq e2 (cdr e))
  (command "break" e1 (car e2) "@")
  (setq e3 (entlast))
  (command "erase" "l" "")
  (setq e4 (entlast))
  (command "oops")
  (command "pedit" e3 "j" e3 e4 "" "")
)
```

To Run:

Type: (load "permsp") <Enter>

Response: C:permsp

Type: PERMSP <Enter>

Response: Select object:

Pick the polyline curve, and it's made permanent.

Length of Arc

Purpose: This program will quickly tell you the length of any arc.

File Name: LARC.LSP

Listing:
```
(defun C:larc ()
  (prompt "\nPick arc: ")
  (setq e1 (car (entsel)))
  (setq e (entget e1))
  (if (= (cdr (assoc 0 ee)) "ARC")
  (progn
  (setq y "Y")
  (command "pedit" e1 "Y" "X")
  (setq e2 (entlast))
  (command "area" "e" e2)
```

```
(command "explode" e2)
)
)
(setq p (getvar "perimeter"))
(setq p (rtos p ))
(princ "\nThe length of the arc is: ")(princ p)
(princ)
)
```

To Run:

Type: (load "larc") <Enter>

Response: C:larc

Type: larc <Enter>

Response: Select object:

Pick the arc. The program will respond with the length.

Explode All Polylines

Purpose: Sometimes you need to communicate with programs that will not accept DXF files with polylines. This program will explode all polylines in a drawing.

File Name: EXPOLY.LSP

Listing:
```
(defun C:expoly ()
  (setq a (ssetget "x" '((0 . "POLYLINE"))))
  (setq len (sslength a))
  (setq ct 0)
  (repeat len
  (setq e (ssname a ct))
  (command "explode" e)
  (setq ct (+ ct 1))
  )
)
```

To Run:

Type: (load "expoly") <Enter>

Response: C:expoly

Type: EXPOLY <Enter>

The program is automatic. All polylines are now exploded.

Copy Layer

Purpose: AutoCAD doesn't have a command to copy objects to another layer, which is often required in order to have a duplicate of the objects on another layer for hatching or taking area measurements. This program not only copies objects to another layer—it makes the layer for you if it does not already exist.

File Name: LCOPY.LSP

Listing:
```
(defun C:Lcopy ()
    (setq layr (getstring "\nEnter target layer name: "))
    (setq a (ssget))
    (command "layer" "n" layr "" )
    (command "copy" a "" "@" "@")
    (command "chprop" a "" "la" layr "" )
)
```

To Run:

Type: (load "Lcopy") <Enter>

Response: C:Lcopy

Type: LCOPY <Enter>

Response: Enter target layer name:

Type: Area <Enter>

Response: Select Objects:

Once the objects are selected, they're copied to the target layer. You can test this out by turning off one layer, moving a group on your drawing or selecting objects and see how many are now selected. It will look as if there's only one set of objects because they're on top of each other.

Stretch Circle

Purpose: This program extends a circle's radius to a point selected by the user. It maintains the center point of the circle. This can be very useful if you need the circle to be tangent to an object.

File Name: STCIRC.LSP

Listing:
```
(defun C:stcirc ()
    (prompt "\nPick circle: ")
    (setq e (entget (car (entsel))))
    (setq pt1 (cdr (assoc 10 e)))
    (setq dis (getdist pt1 "\nPoint distance of radius: "))
    (setq d (assoc 40 e))
    (setq e (subst (cons 40 dis) d e))
    (entmod e)
)
```

To Run:

Type: (load "stcirc") <Enter>

Response: C:stcirc

Type: STCIRC <Enter>

Response: Pick circle:

Pick any point on the circle.

Response: Point distance of radius:

Point to the new radius distance; enter the radius from the keyboard or pick an object you want the circle tangent to.

Last Text

Purpose: When you issue the DTEXT command, the text line following the last text line entered will start with an extra Enter. The problem is that this may not be the line where you want the text to continue. Wouldn't it be nice if you could pick where you want the text to continue? When you select the line of text, you're in the DTEXT command with the text block below the line selected.

File Name: LSTEXT.LSP

Listing:
```
(defun C:lstext ()
    (setq os (getvar "osmode"))
    (setvar "osmode" 64)
    (setq pt1 (getpoint "\nPick the last line of text: "))
    (setvar "osmode" os)
    (command "text" pt1 "" "" "    ")
    (command "dtext" "")
)
```

To Run:

Type: (load "lstext") <Enter>

Response: C:lstext

Type: LSTEXT <Enter>

Response: Pick the last line of text:

Pick any point on a text line. You're automatically Object Snapped to the insertion point. You're now in the DTEXT command, ready to continue on the line below the one you picked.

Caution: This program will work as written only if the text style you're using doesn't have a preset height. If it does, then take out one of the quotation marks in the (command "text" pt1 "" "" "   ") and it will work properly (one " is for height, which is not asked for with preset style).

Save Without .BAK File

Purpose: If you use this way of saving your drawing, you'll not only save the drawing without a backup but you'll also purge the drawing of any unreferenced blocks, linetypes, layers, etc. (But don't use it if you don't want a PURGE All to occur.) It will also tend to make your drawing about 30 percent smaller and more efficient.

File Name: SAVXBAK.LSP

Listing:
```
(defun C:savxbak ()
    (setq a (strcat (getvar "dwgprefix") (getvar "dwgname")))
    (command "wblock" a pause "*")
)
```

To Run:

Type: (load "savxbak") <Enter>

Response: C:savxbak

Type: SAVXBAK <Enter>

> The program is automatic. The drawing will be saved under its own name. Now you must QUIT the drawing. Don't END it or the END will overwrite the drawing without the purges and the .BAK file will be created.

Write Objects to File

Purpose: This program is a quick way to write selected objects to a file—for the purpose of creating a block or simply for writing objects out to disk to segment the drawing. If you don't want a block to be created in the current drawing and want the objects back on the screen, then UNDO 1 after running the program. Even though the creation of the block definition will be undone, the objects are still safely out on disk.

File Name: WRITENT.LSP

Listing:
```
(defun C:writent ()
    (setq filn (getstring "\nName of file: "))
    (setq a (ssget))
    (setq filn1 (strcat filn ".dwg"))
    (if (= nil (findfile filn1))
    (command "wblock" filn "" "0,0" a "")
    (command "wblock" filn pause "" "0,0" a "")
    )
)
```

To Run:

Type: `(load "writent") <Enter>`

Response: `C:writent`

Type: `WRITENT <Enter>`

Response: `Name of file:`

Enter here the name of the target file.

Response: `Select objects:`

Select the objects you want to write to disk and confirm with Enter.

Balloons

Purpose: This program is a quick way to create a balloon (with text in the circle) and a leader line.

File Name: `BALLOON.LSP`

Listing:
```
(defun C:balloon () (graphscr)
   (setq ds (getvar "dimscale"))
   (setq p1 (getpoint "\nFrom point: "))
   (setq p2 (getpoint p1 "\nTo point: "))
   (if (<= (car p2) (car p1)) (setq b (* -0.5 ds))
   (setq b (* 0.5 ds)))
   (setq p3 (list (+ (car p2) b) (cadr p2)))
   (setq p4 (list (+ (car p3) (/ b 2)) (cadr p3)))
   (command "dim1" "leader" p1 p2 p3 ^C ^C)
   (command "circle" p4 (/ (abs b) 2))
   (setq c (getstring 1 "\nText for balloon: "))
   (command "text" "m" p4 (* 0.125 ds) "0" c)
   (princ)
)
```

To Run:

Type: `(load "balloon") <Enter>`

Response: `C:balloon`

Type: `BALLOON <Enter>`

Response: `From point:`

Pick the point where you want the leader arrow to originate.

Response: `To point:`

Pick the point where you want the balloon to be drawn.

Response: `Text for balloon:`

Enter here the text you want in the circle. The text is designed for the middle of the circle. The size of the circle and the text is based on the setting for Dimscale. Of course, all these ratios can be changed.

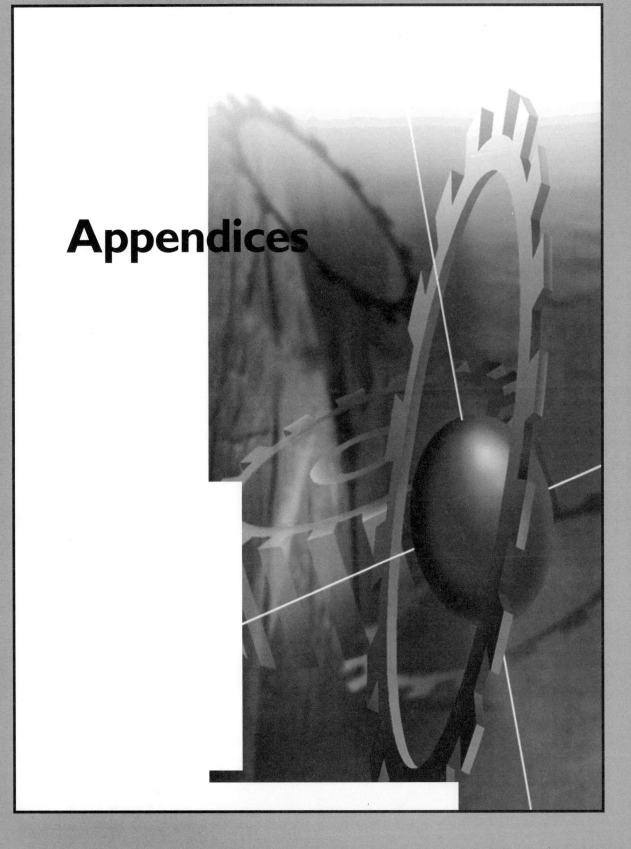

Appendices

Using Text Editors

As you've seen throughout this book, menus, AutoLISP programs and the ACAD.PGP file are simple text files. As such, you work with them through a text editor. There are many commercial text editors on the market, including EDIT in DOS 5.0 and higher as well as Windows Write and Notepad. Each of those has been mentioned in this book.

What text editor are you going to use? There are generally four to choose from. Two of them will work very well, and two of them will not work as well. The four primary possibilities are

- A word processor that you purchased separately for use with Windows.
- Write, a word processor that comes free with Windows. It is generally found in the Accessories program group.
- Notepad, a text editor also found in the Accessories program group.
- The DOS EDIT program. Depending on how your Windows software was installed, EDIT might be under a program icon called MS-DOS Editor. If it's not there you can create it or use the MS-DOS Prompt icon to get to a DOS prompt and then call up EDIT as you would in DOS.

It is universally agreed that Edlin is not the best text editor available. It is not even included on DOS 6.0 and higher. For the most part you should use one of the editors above, but from time to time the menus may be so large that Write, EDIT and Notepad may not have enough memory to handle them. Edlin may be the only way you can edit a large file without a third-party text editor or the dangers of a word processor.

Even though I rarely use Edlin, I carry a copy of it on a utility disk for emergencies when I'm visiting clients. It has been a lifesaver at times when I'm in the field and I have to change a menu file. For these reasons, you should learn how it works, especially its capabilities for working with large files and writing out portions of them.

Following are some suggestions on using each of these text editors.

Word Processors & Write

Which of these is the best and which should you be careful when using? You might have guessed that you probably should be careful when using a word processor, so don't use one unless you have to. Write is OK, but remember that it is a word processor. Word processing programs maintain a hold on the file even if the file is saved to disk. AutoCAD will not be able to load the file and you will get a "file in use" error or a sharing violation error. In Windows you may even get a general protection fault error and risk crashing AutoCAD or Windows itself. Therefore the rule is simple—don't use a Windows word processor or Write to edit your menus unless you have to. For example, your file may be too large for EDIT or Notepad.

When you use Write and start a menu from scratch, make sure you use Save As and then pick Text Only as the file format. Otherwise Write will save the file in its own .WRI format. Remember, it's still a word processor. When you bring an existing menu up using Write, it will ask you if you want to convert the text file. Choose No Conversion.

Notepad

Since Notepad is a Windows program, you might be more inclined to use it. It works very well. When you save the file, Notepad lets go of it so that AutoCAD can load the menu. You can easily toggle back and forth between the windows. Notepad would be the perfect program except that it has no search and replace capability. It has a search routine, but there's no way to globally change anything.

If you use Notepad, make sure the Word Wrap toggle is not checked. It is found under the Edit pull-down menu. If the toggle is checked, the menu file will be word-wrapped based on the size of the window. This can be disastrous.

An advantage to Notepad is that you can copy and paste a program between other Notepad sessions and windows. This is nice if you would like to include a section of an existing menu in a new menu. Just open up two Notepad windows and do a copy and paste between them.

DOS EDIT

DOS EDIT is equally useful. I prefer to run it inside Windows as a windowed program so that I can toggle between the windows. In order to do that you must change the PIF file. Run the Windows PIF Editor and open the EDIT.PIF file. Change the Display Usage from Full Screen to Windowed and save the file. Now when you click on the MS-DOS Editor, you can work in a moveable window.

EDIT's advantage over Notepad is that it does a global search and replace. The disadvantage is that you can copy and paste only within the same EDIT program session. If another program has a segment that you want to use, you must first close out the current file, bring up the file from which you want to copy, highlight and copy the segment, close the current file, bring up the target file and paste. Even though you can bring up multiple sessions of the DOS EDIT program, you can't copy and paste between them as you can with Notepad.

Using Edlin

In the examples that follow, we'll assume that the file to be edited is ACAD.MNU and that you're currently in the AutoCAD directory where ACAD.MNU resides. Begin by entering **EDLIN**, followed by the name of the file to be edited.

Type: `EDLIN ACAD.MNU <Enter>`

You'll receive one of three possible responses. (Notice that in each instance the response for Edlin is an asterisk [*]. Unless instructed otherwise, do not type the asterisk.)

If the file does not exist, the response will be

Response: `New file`
            `*`

This indicates that it's a new file. The * is Edlin's neutral position; it's waiting for the next command.

If the file already exists and is successfully and totally loaded into memory, the response will be

Response: `End of input file`
            `*`

Edlin is saying that since it was able to find the end of the file, the file is completely loaded into Edlin's memory. This means you can work on the entire file at one time. On the other hand, when a file is too big to be loaded into Edlin's memory (as with the ACAD.MNU file), Edlin loads as much text as will fit. If the file exists and is successfully loaded, but only a part of the file was able to fit into memory, the response will be

Response: *

This means that as much of the file as possible has been loaded into memory, but a part of it is still on disk; you can work only on the part that's now loaded into memory. If you need to work on the part that's not currently in memory, you'll have to write the current memory to disk and bring in more of the file until you reach the section you need to work on. Use the A (Append) and W (Write) commands until the file is complete.

Edlin Commands

Let's take a look now at the commands you'll use in Edlin. All Edlin commands are single-letter commands, which can work on either a single line or a group of lines.

L   Lists the first 23 lines or a screen full of information. 14L would list 23 lines, beginning with line 14. 9,14L would list only lines 9 through 14.

I   Inserts a line before all other lines, beginning with line number 1. You continue inserting lines consecutively until you want to end by pressing Ctrl+C. You can begin inserting lines before any existing line number. 14I begins inserting above line 14; the inserted line becomes line 14. Additional inserted lines are consecutively numbered and existing line numbers are moved down and renumbered accordingly.

#D   Deletes a specified line. For example, 14D deletes line 14. All other lines are renumbered accordingly. You may also delete a range of lines: 14,18D will delete lines 14 through 18 inclusive.

If you enter a line number, that line will be displayed and made ready for editing. The line number will appear below the line, followed by an *. If you begin typing, what you type replaces the line; therefore, you can completely replace the line by typing a new line.

You can also position your cursor anywhere in the line by using the F1 function key. Each time you press F1, an existing character of the current line will appear. Press F1 until you're positioned where you want to begin typing. What you type at this point replaces what follows. If you press the Ins (insertion) key, what you type will be inserted, rather than replace existing text. The Delete key deletes forward, but the backspace key doesn't delete backward. Whenever you press Enter, the rest of the line that follows is lost. Function key F3 will print the rest of the line. But be careful; if you fail to press F3 before you press Enter, you could lose the rest of the line.

#,#sXXXX   Especially when working on menus, you'll often need to find a specific pattern in the file. Begin by indicating a range of lines to be searched, followed by the letter "s," for search. Immediately following the letter "s," type in the pattern you want Edlin to look for. The pattern is case-sensitive, so uppercase and lowercase letters must be used in the search pattern exactly as found in the file listing.

For example, if you want to search for ***TABLET1 in the ACAD.MNU file, enter the following:

Type: `1,9999s***TABLET1 <Enter>`

1,9999 is the range of the lines you want searched. This generally means search the entire file, since you'll never have more than 9999 lines in memory at one time. s is the letter used by Edlin to indicate Search. ***TABLET1 is the string you're looking for.

If the search string is not found, Edlin will respond, "Not found." If the search string is found, Edlin responds with the line number the target string is on. If you enter L for LIST, a few lines preceding the target line and a few lines following the target line will list, positioning the target line approximately in the center of the screen.

E   Saves and updates the file and terminates the Edlin session. If all of the file could not be loaded into memory, it will confirm that the entire file has been written out, by terminating with "End of input file." If you don't get this confirmation message during the Edlin session (either when the file is first called up or when it's saved), there may be a problem with the file, and you should take any precautionary measures needed.

When you end an Edlin session and save the file, a backup file is saved as well. Its name is the same as the file name, plus the .BAK extension. If you need to recover this version, you should immediately rename it. Otherwise, the next time you save an Edlin file by the same name, it will write over your current .BAK file.

Q   This aborts all changes you've made to the file and exits Edlin. You'll be asked whether you want to abort any edits, Y or N. If you enter **Y**, you'll exit Edlin without saving any changes you made.

Insufficient Memory

If an entire file fits into memory, you'll get the "End of input file" message. If a portion of the file cannot load, you'll get only an *. You can still work with the entire file in a forward direction only. Enter the W command, and Edlin writes the current portion of the file to disk. Then enter the A command, and Edlin appends as much of the rest of the file as it can:

Type: W <Enter>
       A <Enter>

You can continue to use W and A in sequence until you find the portion of the file you need to work on. Remember, this is a one-way street. You can't go back. When you END (E Enter), the entire file is written to disk. If you do need to go back to the beginning of the file, you must end the file and begin Edlin again. It will take several W's and A's to go through the entire file.

W and A in sequence without any line numbers in front of the W will write all the current file into memory, and A will read in as much of the rest of the file as possible. This is the standard way to page through the file until you find the area of the file you want to work with.

You may not always want to write out all of the lines currently in memory, since you may need to refer back to preceding file portions. To write out only a portion of the lines currently in memory, you can enter a number in front of the W. The following command writes out only the first 50 lines in memory:

Type: 50w <Enter>

This will make enough room in memory to insert some more lines. Then you can use the W and A sequence until the entire file is saved.

Be very careful using this method. The line numbers aren't constant; they change whenever new lines are inserted. Therefore, these numbers represent relative line order only at a given point in time.

Using AutoLISP

More and more, AutoLISP is becoming a powerful substitute for Auto-CAD's macro language in the menu structure. AutoLISP is not difficult to learn, but you must become familiar with the language. Once you invest the time, the rewards never end. This appendix is not designed to teach you how to write AutoLISP programs. *AutoLISP in Plain English* (also published by Ventana Press) does a good job of that. The purpose here is to focus on turning AutoLISP routines and functions into menu macros, and using AutoLISP from the AutoCAD command line or directly from the AutoCAD menu.

Loading & Executing AutoLISP

An AutoLISP program is entered as a regular text file. Therefore you will use the same type of text editor that you have been using for your menus. An AutoLISP program is stored in a file with the .LSP extension. Before the program can be run, it must be loaded into memory. Let's assume the name of the file is LISP1.LSP and the name of the program is C:prog1. The C: in front of the program name lets you run the program the same way you'd enter any AutoCAD command—by typing in its name.

To load the program, begin at the AutoCAD command line.

Type: (load "lisp1") <Enter>

Once the program is loaded, you can run it by entering **prog1** and pressing Enter. Don't put a C: in front of the program name when you're running the program. That is used only in the program itself to designate that it can be used on the same level as any other AutoCAD command. AutoLISP accepts either uppercase or lowercase code. In a DOS or Windows environment it doesn't matter which case you use. But if you're running on a UNIX-based machine, UNIX is case sensitive. So if the file name is in uppercase, you must input that file in uppercase. Otherwise UNIX won't recognize that name.

But if you're a DOS or Windows user, what happens if the file you want to load is in a different directory? You can specify the path to the file's location. But in order to maintain AutoLISP compatibility in UNIX environments, AutoCAD requires that the slashes used to designate the directory be forward slashes (/), regardless of the operating system. Therefore, to load a file in the \LISP directory called LISP1, you would

Type: `(load "C:/lisp/lisp1") <Enter>`

Each program is a function or a collection of functions. Unlike BASIC and some other languages, the (program) function and the file that contains it aren't one and the same. In fact, one file may contain many functions. Whenever you load a file, all functions in that file are available to you. Each function must begin with the statement "(defun" and end with a closing parenthesis. This sets the function limits.

AutoCAD Commands in AutoLISP

Most of what you'll be doing with AutoLISP in menus is issuing AutoCAD commands at the menu level. This is accomplished with AutoLISP's "(command)". Here's how it works.

You can issue virtually any AutoCAD command from inside AutoLISP. Begin the expression with (command followed by the AutoCAD command in quotes. All of the required entries must be provided in a (command expression. If the user supplies some of the entries, the word pause must be used where these entries would come. Look at the following example: it inserts a block at a user-specified point, using a 1 to 1 scale and 0 rotation.

`(command "insert" "part1" pause "1" "1" "0")`

You'll use such an expression many times in your menus. The expression is begun with a (command. "insert" is the AutoCAD command you want to issue. "part1" is the name of the block. pause gives the user the opportunity to pick the insertion point. "1" "1" is what you would type in if you were answering the insertion questions yourself. You might think you would just press Enter twice. This may be the case, but an Enter sets a 1 to 1 scale if that was the last default. So it's generally better to be precise in AutoLISP and give the exact scale for X and Y. Of course, if you wanted it to be placed at a .5 scale, you'd put in ".5" ".5" instead. Notice that the entry is made with quotation marks. If you type something from the keyboard, it should almost always be put in as a quoted string rather than a numeric value without quotes. Putting the numerics in an incorrect format is a common mistake in AutoLISP, so it's better to type in quoted strings, exactly as you would in AutoCAD.

The "0" represents the rotation of the part. Again, it is input as a quoted string. If you want to, you can replace the "0" with a pause. This would let the user position the rotation.

Remember that all AutoLISP expressions must begin and end with opening and closing parentheses.

Inline AutoLISP

One of the things you need to watch out for is that AutoCAD puts a lot of AutoLISP inline code in the AutoCAD menu. Although you may be tempted to do so, you shouldn't add to it by placing large programs in the menu structure itself. Generally, when you write a program, it's better to place it out on disk, then simply access the program from a single-line menu entry. This not only helps to keep the AutoCAD menu file as small as possible; it also makes your program accessible from the menu and from the keyboard as well.

Toolbar Buttons

Remember that toolbars are the one type of menu that will not let you use simple menu statements. You cannot enter $I=MYIMAGE $I=*. This is menu language. In reality the toolbar buttons are not part of the menu, even though they are eventually stored in the menu. Therefore you must either place a regular AutoCAD command in the Macro box or an Auto-LISP command or program.

Menu Loading

A problem you may run into is that the program must be loaded from the file before it can be executed. Now, you could put all your programs in the ACAD.LSP file, but it would be a time-consuming ordeal to load that file each time you go into the drawing editor. On the other hand, you don't want to load a file that's already been loaded, since this too can waste a lot of time. Here's the solution:

Assume that the name of the program you want to execute is prog1 in a file called LISP1. This is the line you would put in the ACAD.MNU file in order to execute the program:

```
^C^C(if (not prog1)(load "lisp1"))(C:prog1)
```

The ^C^C cancels any command that might be in effect. The name of the program follows *not*. The file is loaded, not the function. Without this command, the file would have to be loaded each time a function is used. With this command, the file won't be loaded if the function is already active. Whether or not the file is loaded, you still want to execute the program. *(C:prog1)* executes the program. If the program were written with a C: in front of the program name, then the C: must be placed with the program's name in parentheses. If the program was not written with a C:, you put only the name of the program in parentheses. In any event, the name of the program must be within parentheses when accessed from a menu or AutoLISP program.

About the Online Companion

Ventana Online is an Internet site created to offer information, software and support for computer users and customers of Ventana Communications (the publisher of this book). Ventana Online is breaking new ground by offering, through the Internet, the *AutoCAD Online Companion*, a never-ending source of valuable information.

The *AutoCAD Online Companion* is an informative tool, as well as an annotated archive of free AutoCAD programs found on the Internet. It also offers an archive of Ventana AutoCAD utilities for sale and provides links to other Internet AutoCAD references, including newsgroups covering AutoCAD tips and tricks, and e-mail mailing lists where you can meet with other AutoCAD professionals to discuss cool new trends and the latest secrets of the trade.

Perhaps one of the most impressive features of the online companion is its Software Archive. Here, you'll find and be able to download the latest versions of all the software mentioned in books in Ventana's AutoCAD Reference Library that are freely available on the Net.

The *AutoCAD Online Companion* also links you to the Ventana Library, where you will find useful press and jacket information, as well as other Ventana Press offerings. Plus you have access to a wide selection of exciting new releases and coming attractions. In addition, Ventana's Online Library allows you to order online the books you want.

The *AutoCAD Online Companion* represents Ventana Online's ongoing commitment to offering the most dynamic and exciting products possible. And soon Ventana Online will be adding more services, including more multimedia supplements, searchable indices and sections of the book reproduced and hyperlinked to the Internet resources they reference.

To access the online companion, connect via the World Wide Web to **http://www.vmedia.com/autocad.html**.

Further Reading

Elliot, Steven D., Ronald W. Leigh, and Brian Matthews. *AutoCAD: A Concise Guide to Commands & Features*. Fourth edition. Chapel Hill, NC: Ventana Press, 1995.

Head, George O. *AutoCAD 3D Companion*. Second edition. Chapel Hill, NC: Ventana Press, 1995.

Head, George O. *AutoLISP in Plain English*. Fifth edition. Chapel Hill, NC: Ventana Press, 1995.

Head, George O., and Jan Doster Head. *1000 AutoCAD Tips & Tricks*. Fourth edition. Chapel Hill, NC: Ventana Press, 1995.

Colophon

This book was produced with PageMaker 5.0 on a Macintosh Quadra. Page proofs were printed on an Hewlett-Packard LaserJet Printer. The output to film was on a Linotronic 330 imagesetter. The body type is Palatino 11/13.5. The headlines are set in DTC Classical Sans. All code is set in Letter Gothic.

The AutoCAD Reference Library

The AutoCAD 3D Companion, Second Edition 🌐
$34.95, 648 pages, illustrated, includes companion disk

Master AutoCAD's complex 3D capabilities with advice from veteran AutoCAD author George O. Head. This definitive guide examines all 3D features, with examples and practical applications. Fully updated for Release 13 for Windows, with a special section on Autovision, the rendering and texture mapping facility from 3D Studio. The companion disk includes all the featured AutoLISP programs from the "3D Toolkit."

AutoCAD: A Concise Guide to Commands & Features, Fourth Edition 🌐
$27.95, 696 pages, illustrated, includes companion disk

Everything you need to produce drawings with AutoCAD—all the key commands, features and skills—is at your fingertips. Highlighted by hands-on exercises, 45 clear, concise chapters lead you from the simple to the complex. The companion disk contains drawings from exercises in the book, productivity-enhancing AutoLISP routines and more!

The AutoCAD Reference Library Deluxe CD-ROM 🌐
$99.95

AutoCAD users spend most of their working days on the computer. Now, that's where the help is! For the first time on CD-ROM, all five books in the Ventana series are online, fully indexed and searchable by topic, title and keyword. Follow references to a given topic from title to title, or page through general subjects. All the programs, routines and support files from the books are included in this innovative digital handbook.

Ride the Windows Wave

The Windows Internet Tour Guide, Second Edition 🌐

$29.95, 424 pages, illustrated, includes companion disk

This runaway bestseller has been updated to include Ventana Mosaic™, the hot new Web reader, along with graphical software for e-mail, file downloading, newsreading and more. Noted for its down-to-earth documentation, the new edition features expanded listings and a look at new Net developments.

America Online's Internet, Windows Edition

$24.95, 328 pages, illustrated, includes companion disk

AOL members can now slide onto the Infobahn with a mere mouse click. This quick-start for AOL Interent newcomers explains e-mail, downloading files, reading newsgroups and joining mailing lists. The companion disk includes AOL software and 10 hours of free online time (for new members only).

Mosaic Quick Tour for Windows, Special Edition 🌐

$24.95, 224 pages, illustrated,
includes two companion disks

A national bestseller straight out of the gate in its first edition, thanks to its down-to-earth approach to Mosaic™—the "killer app" that changed the face of the Internet. The Web, with its audio, video and graphic capabilities and hyperlinks between sites, comes to life in this important update that focuses on Ventana Mosaic™, the newly standardized commercial version of the most famous free software in the world. Includes information on audio and video components of Ventana Mosaic, along with a guide to top Web attractions. Two companion disks feature Ventana Mosaic and Win32s required to run the program.

Looking Good in Print, Third Edition
$24.95, 464 pages, illustrated

For use with any software or hardware, this desktop design bible has become the standard among novice and experienced desktop publishers alike. Now with more than 300,000 copies in print, *Looking Good in Print, Third Edition,* is even better—including new sections on photography and scanning. Learn the fundamentals of professional-quality design along with tips on resources and reference materials.

Windows, Word & Excel Office Companion, Second Edition
$21.95, 694 pages, illustrated

With more than 100,000 copies sold, this groundbreaking title eliminates the need for newcomers to purchase three separate books. Three sections offer easy introductions to Microsoft's industry-leading software: Windows™ through Version 3.1, Word through Version 6 and Excel through Version 5. An extensive index makes this down-to-earth guide to basic commands and features an easy reference that saves time, money and valuable desktop acreage.

The Visual Guide to Paradox for Windows
$29.95, 692 pages, illustrated, includes companion disk

Whether you're a DOS veteran or a newcomer to Paradox, this *Visual Guide* will help you with your Windows database management and programming. Covers all the new graphical capabilities of Windows as well as the latest features of Paradox, including the graphic Query Editor, BOCA (Borland Object Component Architecture) and ObjectPAL, Paradox's new object-oriented program language. The companion disk includes all the macros, reports, tables and queries needed to create an initial working database.

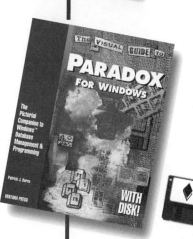

WHAT'S THE NEXT BIG THING ON THE NET?

Version 2.0 of Ventana Media's *Internet Membership Kit.*

More software. More value. More possibilities.

The **ALL-IN-ONE SOLUTION** for Internet Access.

Version 2.0 delivers **EVERYTHING** you need to get started:

- Sign up with one-button access to IBM Internet Connection, the world's most reliable service provider. Registration fee waived!

- Send and receive messages all over the world in seconds via e-mail!

- Explore the World Wide Web with Ventana Mosaic™, a licensed version of the most popular Web browser.

- Download files from around the globe using file transfer software (FTP) and Gopher!

- Keep up to date with software and listings on Ventana Online with the FREE *Online Companion*™.

You also receive the most innovative listings guide to the Internet, *Internet Roadside Attractions,* featuring WebWalker™: a hyperlinked CD-ROM that provides live links to Internet sites when you log onto the Net! Plus the bestselling *Internet Tour Guide*, the easiest, most complete guide to your Internet software.

SPECIAL BONUS: A one-year subscription to Ventana's *Online Companion*™, featuring software, online listings updated daily and a one-stop Internet Help Center.

One box. One solution. A virtually infinite way of communicating, from Ventana.

To order any Ventana Press title, complete this order form and mail or fax it to us, with payment, for quick shipment.

TITLE	ISBN	Quantity		Price		Total
1000 AutoCAD Tips & Tricks, 4th Edition	1-56604-141-4	_____	x	$34.95	=	$ _____
America Online's Internet, Windows Edition	1-56604-176-7	_____	x	$24.95	=	$ _____
The AutoCAD 3D Companion, 2nd Edition	1-56604-142-2	_____	x	$34.95	=	$ _____
AutoCAD: A Concise Guide, 4th Edition	1-56604-139-2	_____	x	$27.95	=	$ _____
The AutoCAD Productivity Book, 6th Ed.	1-56604-185-6	_____	x	$34.95	=	$ _____
The AutoCAD Reference Library Deluxe CD-ROM	1-56604-226-7	_____	x	$99.95	=	$ _____
AutoLISP in Plain English, 5th Edition	1-56604-140-6	_____	x	$27.95	=	$ _____
The Internet Membership Kit, Macintosh Version 2.0	1-56604-213-5	_____	x	$69.95	=	$ _____
The Internet Membership Kit, Windows Version 2.0	1-56604-212-7	_____	x	$69.95	=	$ _____
Looking Good in Print, 3rd Edition	1-56604-047-7	_____	x	$24.95	=	$ _____
Mosaic Quick Tour for Windows, Special Edition	1-56604-214-3	_____	x	$24.95	=	$ _____
The Visual Guide to Paradox for Windows	1-56604-150-3	_____	x	$29.95	=	$ _____
The Windows Internet Tour Guide, 2nd Edition	1-56604-174-0	_____	x	$29.95	=	$ _____
Windows, Word & Excel Desktop Companion, 2nd Edition	1-56604-083-3	_____	x	$21.95	=	$ _____

Subtotal = $ _____

Shipping = $ _____

TOTAL = $ _____

SHIPPING:

For all standard orders, please ADD $4.50/first book, $1.35/each additional.
For Internet Membership Kit orders, ADD $6.50/first kit, $2.00/each additional.
For "two-day air," ADD $8.25/first book, $2.25/each additional.
For "two-day air" on the kits, ADD $10.50/first book, $4.00/each additional.
For orders to Canada, ADD $6.50/book.
For orders sent C.O.D., ADD $4.50 to your shipping rate.
North Carolina residents must ADD 6% sales tax.
International orders require additional shipping charges.

Name _____   Daytime telephone _____

Company _____

Address (No PO Box) _____

City_____   State_____ Zip _____

____ Payment enclosed ____VISA ____ MC Acc't # _____ Exp. date_____

Signature _____ Exact name on card _____

Mail to: Ventana Press, PO Box 2468, Chapel Hill, NC 27515 ☎ 800/743-5369 Fax 919/942-1140